at home with the makers of style

grant scott and samantha scott-jeffries
with 218 illustrations in colour

contents

First published in the United Kingdom in 2005 by
Thames & Hudson Ltd, 181A High Holborn, London WC1V 7QX

www.thamesandhudson.com

British Library Cataloguing-in-Publication Data
A catalogue record for this book is available from the British Library

ISBN-13: 978-0-500-51234-0
ISBN-10: 0-500-51234-5

Printed and bound in China by C&C Offset Printing Co., Ltd.

introduction

Never before has design been so important in our everyday lives, or our decision-making so affected by aesthetic choice. We fill our homes with products that say as much about us as what we wear. We embrace the vast consumer choice that is available to us and often base our purchasing decisions on the way an object looks, not on how it functions or how much we need it. We are more design-aware than ever before and we are able to choose from a never-ending supply of styles. Yet we know relatively little about the names that mould our tastes or set the design agenda. Who are the people who exert such an influence over the way that we live today? Who are the men and women responsible for designing the razor we shave with, the chair that we sit on, or the hotel that we stay in? And when we probe to find the person behind the brand, what do we discover about how they choose to live? Do they practise what they preach? The answers to these questions are not straightforward, but are explored through the photographs and the designer's own words within this book. Their own homes are surprising, eclectic, highly creative and very personal. Some of their owners believe so fervently in their vision that they have filled their homes with objects from their own imagination. Others have invested in classic pieces designed by their heroes, past and present. Full of conflicting opinions and the unexpected, this book shows how the design icons of the 21st century live, their thoughts on design and their dreams for the future.

Education Alessi graduated in Milan in 1970 with a degree in law.
Career Alessi joined the family business in 1970 and developed
worldwide contacts with international designers and architects.
He is now the Managing Director and General Manager of Alessi
Spa and is in charge of Marketing Strategy, Communication and
Design Management. **Awards** In 1998 he received the Design
Award for Lifetime Achievement from the Brooklyn Museum of
Art, New York. **Further information** Alessi has written three
books, *La Cintura di Orione* in 1986, *Not in Production, Next to
Production* in 1988 and *The Dream Factory* also in 1988. He
has collaborated with numerous international magazines and
publications on articles about design and he is a visiting professor
at several design colleges. He is a member of the academic board
of the UIAH (University of Art and Design), Helsinki, Finland, and
of the honorary committee of the Design Museum, London. He
is a Senior Fellow of the Royal College of Art, London, Honorary
Professor of the Hochschule der Bildenden Künste, Saarbrucken,
Germany, as well as Doctor Honoris Causa of the UIAH (University
of Art and Design), Helsinki, Finland, and Doctor of Fine Arts at the
Miami University of Oxford, Ohio. He was awarded an Honorary
Doctorate from the University of Central England, Birmingham,
in 2001.

alberto
alessi

This house may seem like a dilapidated ruin, but in the eyes of Alberto Alessi it is the culmination of twenty-five years of desire. The views out over Lake Orta, just one hour north of Milan, speak for themselves. The house and vineyard will not be completed for many years, but as he stands in the grounds looking into the distance, you can tell that Alessi can see the finished result very clearly.

"Alberto, I've a wonderful idea for you."

Right The main winery and new entrance will be located on this side of the house. **Below right** The main building is an unsafe structure even though there are still two tenants living in the rear of the building. **Below left** Today, the decorative arch and entrance to the inner courtyard are surrounded by waist-high vegetation. **Opposite** Alessi believes that it will be approximately two years before his home is habitable.

"I've learnt that there is a fight, in human beings, between technology and poetry."

Opposite In the main building the windows are covered with corrugated metal sheeting and a sign that reads 'Vietato entrare' (No entry); 'Solette pericolanti' (Unsafe paving stones); 'La proprietà declina ogni responsabilità in caso di accesso non autorizzato' (The owner will not be held responsible in the event of unauthorized access). **Above right** Alessi standing under the arch that leads to the inner courtyard. **Right** The view from the house out over Lake Orta, towards the island of San Giulio.

015

"Design is meant to be sold."

A redeveloped undertakers and mortuary on a main street in Manhattan's Alphabet City is where you will find Harry Allen's first-floor apartment. The entrance hall retains the original marble floor and walls, but upstairs is very much the home of a sophisticated New Yorker. Filled with his own work design classics and pieces from close friends, Allen lives with his partner John and their two basset hounds.

"I believe that if you assemble a group of beautiful, interesting things all together they will become a beautiful, decorative scheme and will speak of the inhabitant, the collector."

Opposite A Donald Judd
wooden chair sits on top of the
marble-topped sideboard; the
sculpture is by Sol LeWitt. The
framed digital print of a moth
was taken by the American
photographer Joseph Scheer.
Right Allen seated in front of
a shelving system he designed
himself. On the table are three
candlesticks, also by him,
which were cast from found
objects. **Below right** Detail
of an Eames chair for Herman
Miller with an Eiffel Tower base.

"I like light and organization."

03.

Education Shin Azumi: awarded a Masters in industrial design at the Royal College of Art, London, and a Bachelor of Arts in product design at Kyoto City University of Art, Japan. Tomoko Azumi: awarded a Masters in furniture design at the Royal College of Art, London, and a Bachelor of Arts in environmental design at Kyoto City University of Art, Japan. **Career** Shin and Tomoko formed Azumi in London after leaving the Royal College of Art in 1995. Their particular interpretation of the simplicity of form normally associated with Japanese design, with a European sense of humour and fluidity of line, has brought them international acclaim and success. Always exploring new areas of design across a product, furniture, space and technology related environment, their aim is to push the horizon and blur the boundaries of design. **Awards** Azumi was awarded the Product of the Year FX International Design Award, UK, in 2000; the Best Furniture FX International Design Award, UK, and Good Design Award, JIDPO (Japan Industrial Design Promotion Organization), Japan, in 2001; the Best Public Lighting FX International Design Award, UK, in 2002; the Best Public Seating FX International Design Award, UK, and Best Contribution at the 100% Design Blueprint Award, UK, in 2003; and in 2004 they were short listed for the Jerwood Applied Design Prize by the Crafts Council, UK. **Clients** Include Isokon PLUS, Authentics, Habitat, Desalto, Benchmark and Guzzini. **Further information** The entertaining aspects of the Azumis' designs have come from their experiences as director and art director of the dance company, Vital Theatre, at the Edinburgh Festival in 1993.

azumis

Among the overcrowded streets of deepest East London there is a place of sophisticated, peaceful calm. A space of considered taste, filled with refined design, simple materials and a brilliant light, it is the home of Shin and Tomoko Azumi.

"Design is a means to a purpose, with a grace to its existence."

Right A collection of pebbles and fossils, together with a plastic extrusion material experiment by the Azumis. **Below right** The view into the bedroom area from the library corridor. The 'Table=Chest' set as a chest in the foreground is by the Azumis as is the 'Stool=Shelf' next to the bed. The sofa, also by the Azumis, is for Hitch Mylius. **Below left** Looking from the mezzanine lounge into the bedroom. Against the far wall is another Azumi piece entitled 'Bench=Bed'; they also designed the rug for E&Y. The 'Table=Chest' is set as a table. **Opposite** The first floor is one large, open space which acts as a bedroom, a library and a lounge. The use of blinds, fabric screens and steel and glass doors all designed by the Azumis allows each area to either be closed off and separated from or open to the mezzanine lounge which looks down over their studio area. The white stool from Habitat was designed by Sori Yanagi in 1954. The Azumis designed the shelves.

"Bright, open, ordered and functional."

Opposite The Azumis sourced and handbuilt the wall covered in off-cut timber at Benchmark Furniture; it also houses the doorway to the bathroom. The 7ft-long table is by the Azumis and the chairs are by Fritz Hansen. **Left** The kitchen preparation surface is home to a collection of the Azumis' designs which they use and test on a daily basis. The bread bin is part of a collection called 'La Tina' for Guzzini and the 'Snowman' porcelain salt and pepper pots, and oil and vinegar bottles are for Authentics. **Below left** A half-height wall divides the kitchen from the studio area; it is also a wall of office storage on one side and kitchen storage on the other. The stacking 'Stool=Shelf' in the foreground is by the Azumis. **Below right** The bedroom area is flanked on one side by a bank of walnut veneered wardrobes which link the bedroom to the library corridor. The fabric screen can be pulled across the space to close off the bedroom.

Clinging to the side of a mountain overlooking San Francisco Bay, Behar's upside-down, three-storey home is filled with light and Californian calm. Hummingbirds swoop past the balcony and the surrounding giant redwoods are protected by law. Behar completed most of the work on the house himself.

"Look inside before looking outside."

Below top left The kitchen area leads off both the dining area and the lounge. In the foreground are 'LEM' high stools by Shin and Tomoko Azumi. **Below top right** Designed by Behar, the entrance area to the house has a wooden retaining wall which echoes the slope of the roof. Behar found the iron chair at Trout Farm in Berkeley and, although reminiscent of a piece by Harry Bertoia, it seems more likely to have been made by a highly skilled amateur. **Below bottom right** The dining area looks out towards the front of the house. The floor standing light in the corner is by Gae Aulenti for Artemide. **Below bottom left** Detail of the wall painted by artist Kameron Gad. **Opposite** The dividing wall between the entrance hallway and the dining area was painted by artist Kameron Gad, a friend of Behar from New York who was inspired by the landscape surrounding the house. Pablo Pardo designed the roll-up screen Ventana light. The central ceiling light above the table is a 1950s Austrian design; the table is by George Nelson and the chairs are by Charles and Ray Eames for Herman Miller. The additional chairs were designed by Martin Van Severen for Vitra. On the table is a Ron Arad black vase and a 1970s Sony portable projection TV.

"A house is a meeting point, where friends and family gather for a shared experience."

Opposite Made of beech wood, the organic wooden chair was found at Trout Farm in Berkeley by Behar. **Above right** The shelving and storage that runs the length of the lounge area is by B&B Italia and was designed by Antonio Citterio. In the foreground the sculptural wooden jigsaw is by Enzo Mari for Danese. The grey box and white plastic ellipse are both copies of the magazine *Visionaire*. **Above left** The main lounge area looks out over San Francisco Bay. Situated in front of the windows, the large oval sculptural piece is an electoluminescent light called Inner Light and was originally designed by Behar for the San Francisco Museum of Modern Art. The chair in the corner is a laser-cut plywood prototype of a chair by Stew Design and the photograph on the wall is a digital snapshot by Behar which he uses to hide the television. The large, soft sheep-skin seating cushion, made in Argentina, is Behar's favourite place to sit. The sage green rug is by Kasthall and the petrol blue sofa is by James Irvine for B&B Italia. **Left** Looking from the lounge towards the kitchen area. The 'RAR' chairs in the foreground are by Charles and Ray Eames and were purchased by Behar when he was still a student. In the background two Chinese opium mats are used to display a Moroccan couscous bowl and a plastic bowl by James Dyson.

Left The bedside table is by Raymond Loewy and the television is a 1970s JVC. **Below left** A detail of the en suite bathroom. On the shelf crafted by Jessie Madsen is a 'Spacescent' perfume bottle designed by Behar. **Opposite** Behar designed the en suite bathroom off his bedroom and used a penny-round tile which covers the floor and walls, including inside the full-length shower. The LCW chair by the translucent glass sliding doors is by Charles and Ray Eames.

"We found each other…she was a mess, I was one too…there was some fixing to do…"

05.

Education Ronan Bouroullec: studied at the Ecole Nationale des Arts Décoratifs, Paris, France. Erwan Bouroullec: studied at the Ecole des Beaux-Arts, Cergy-Pontoise, France. **Career** After graduating, Ronan began working alone, but collaborated more and more with his brother, Erwan, who was still a student at the time. The two brothers have been working together officially since 1999. In 1997 they met Giulio Cappellini while showing their 'Disintegrated Kitchen' at the Salon du Meuble in Paris. This was the beginning of a strong and creative partnership that continues today. In 2000 Issey Miyake commissioned them to create his new shop in Paris and in the same year they met Rolf Fehlbaum, Chairman of Vitra, and began working on a new office furniture system called 'Joyn'. **Awards** The Bouroullec brothers were named 'Creator of the Year' at the Salon du Meuble in Paris, 2002, and have won many other awards such as Le Grand prix du design de la ville de Paris in 1998, the First Prize of the Saint-Etienne Biennale in 1998 and the New Designer Awards of the International Furniture Fair of New York in 1999. In 2003 they were elected Designer of the Year by *Elle Decoration*, Japan. **Clients** Include Vitra, Cappellini, Issey Miyake, Magis, Ligne Roset and Habitat. **Further information** After the first publication dedicated to their work, *Ronan et Erwan Bouroullec – Catalogue de Raison* in 2002, they designed their first monograph, *Ronan and Erwan Bouroullec*, published in 2003. Both brothers regularly take part in various Art School workshops and Ronan is a professor at the Ecole Cantonale d'Art de Lausanne in Switzerland.

the bpouro ullec brothers

"We keep our eyes wide open."

In a northern suburb of Paris, hidden next to a car repair shop,
Ronan and Erwan Bouroullec work and spend all of their time.
There is no sign on the nondescript wooden door to reveal what
occurs inside. The entrance smells, feels and looks more like
a long-forgotten hardware store – this is a true workshop,
without any pretence or glamour.

Opposite A close-up detail of the Bouroullecs' note book, cigarettes and desk. **Above right** A screen designed by the Bouroullecs in 2002. **Above left** The carpet tiles entitled 'Piece of Carpet' were created for Sommer, France. **Left** Two examples of the Hole chairs designed by the Bouroullecs for Cappellini.

"The foundation of design is for us a question of context."

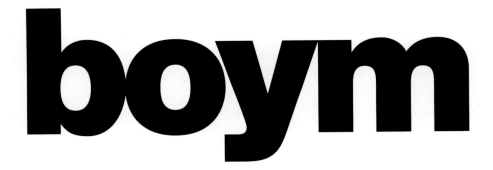

06.

Education Constantin Boym: studied at the Moscow Architectural Institute and was also awarded a Masters degree in design from the Domus Academy in Milan. Laurene Leon Boym: awarded a Bachelor of Fine Arts from the School of Visual Arts, New York, and a Masters in industrial design from the Pratt Institute, New York. **Career** Constantin moved to New York in 1986 and founded Boym Partners Inc. with his wife Laurene who was the Designer-in-Residence at the Cooper-Hewitt, National Design Museum at the Smithsonian in Washington, D.C., from 1998 to 2001. Together they worked on a three-year long catalogue project entitled 'Souvenirs for the End of the Century'. Objects from the catalogue were included in 'The American Century' exhibition at the Whitney Museum of American Art, New York, in 1999 and in the National Design Triennial at the Cooper-Hewitt, National Design Museum, Washington, D.C., in 2000. They continue to work in New York on a wide variety of projects. **Awards** A book about the work of the Boym Partners, *Curious Boym: Design Works*, was published in 2002 and received the *ID Magazine* Design Award in 2003. **Clients** Include Alessi, Authentics, Swatch and Vitra. **Further information** Constantin Boym is the author of *New Russian Design*, published in 1992. From 1989 to 2000 he was a professor and program co-ordinator at the Parsons School of Design in New York. Laurene Leon Boym was a founder of the Association of Women Industrial Designers in 1992, she co-curated 'Goddess in the Details', an exhibition organized by the Association of Women Industrial Designers, in 1995 and ran the organization between 1995 and 1997. She currently teaches product design at the Parsons School of Design, New York.

"Our projects reflect everyday aspects of American lifestyle and landscape."

The Boym family live in a solid, red brick building built like a fortress around a central fountain the size of a municipal swimming pool on the Lower East Side of Manhattan. It is a home that resounds to the noise of loud music and the Boyms' eight-year-old son Bobby. Each of the three rooms in their apartment has a very different design sense, but Laurene's passion for tidiness is the linking factor.

Right Miniature buildings collected by the Boyms on their travels. **Below right** A framed triptych, entitled 'Sears is Hot', by Russian artists Komar and Melamid. **Below left** In the living room the 'Strap' chair was designed by Boym for Vitra and the small gnome stool/table is Philippe Starck for Kartell. **Opposite** In the home office, the tan leather chair is by Charles and Ray Eames, the diamond metal wire chairs are by Harry Bertoia and the white shelving is from IKEA. The ceiling light is from a store on the Bowery, Manhattan.

"I like the rooms with the pale-coloured vignettes – it is as if they were stage sets or memories of other imaginary apartments."

Above left and above right Very much Laurene's space, the bedroom is home to her collection of J. H. Lynch paintings which she regularly changes. The 'Knotted chair' is by Marcel Wanders and the central ceiling light is by DMD/Droog Design. **Opposite** The light in the home office is a one-off art piece by Arman.

"We like to have fun with the environment and the room themes often change. I decided on 'hedonism' for the bedroom."

07.

Career Busnelli founded his first company, which produced armchairs, in northern Italy in 1953 and in 1966 he started C&B Italia with Cesare Cassina. He collaborated with some of the very best Italian furniture designers of the time such as Gio Ponti and Vico Magistretti. In 1964, while in London, Busnelli became interested in the production of cold-formed polyurethane and developed his own processes which he refined and began using in the large-scale mass production of furniture. In 1973 he took over the complete running of the company and renamed it B&B Italia. In the 1970s and 1980s his sons started to take over the day-to-day running of the company. Then in 1990, at the age of sixty-five, Busnelli decided to start a new company, B&B Italia Marine, which designs and refits the interiors of large, ocean-going ships.

piero
busnelli

"I don't like working with a personal computer, or with a pen. I prefer observing."

As the electrically operated steel gates slowly open, young deer bound through the long grass and ducks sit contentedly in the middle of the gravel track. This is Piero Busnelli's retreat – a place to be alone and look back on his life. He started hunting when he was twenty-two years old and this is where he keeps his trophies. Opinions are divided and strongly held concerning such a pastime, but as Busnelli says, 'today, I really prefer my animals alive!'

Left The stairwell up to the bedrooms is home to Busnelli's oceanic conquests. **Below left** Busnelli peering out of the front door. **Opposite** The main entrance hall gives little idea of the contents of Busnelli's retreat, but ensures an elegant and sympathetic transition from the surrounding parkland.

"The suitable solution is always to find the right balance."

"Taste is to be able to place objects and furniture so that everything works perfectly."

Above left A large map of the world in the entrance hall is covered with small pins indicating all of Busnelli's hunting expeditions. **Above right** Detail of the main hall. **Opposite** In the main hall the B&B Italia furniture contrasts with over two hundred animals all of which were hunted by Busnelli.

08.

Education Fernando Campana: awarded a Bachelor of Arts in architecture at the Faculdade de Belas Artes de São Paulo in Brazil. Humberto Campana: awarded a Bachelor of Arts in law at the Universidade de São Paulo in Brazil. **Career** After a series of industrial design teaching positions at the Fundação Armando Alvares Penteado in his native São Paulo, and despite his training in law, Humberto decided to join forces with his brother Fernando to form The Campana Brothers. Fernando had also been teaching industrial design at the Fundação Armando Alvares Penteado and at the Museu Brasileiro de Escultura (the Brazilian Museum of Sculpture). Their mixed educational backgrounds, industrial design experience and understanding of modern Brazil has brought them international acclaim with a wide variety of designs ranging from chairs to desk tidies. **Awards** In 1992 they were awarded the Aquisição Award by the Museu de Arte Brasileira (Museum of Brazilian Art); in 1996, the First Prize Design Award at the XXI Salão de Arte de Ribeirão Preto, Brazil; in 1997, First Prize for Residential Furniture; in 1999 they were awarded the prestigious George Nelson Design Award, USA, and in 2001, the Special Prize Award from the Museu da Casa Brasileira (Museum of the Brazilian House), São Paulo, Brazil, for packaging for a H. Stern jewelry collection. **Clients** Include Edra, Alessi, Museum of Modern Art, New York, ACME, Fontana Arte and Cappellini. **Further information** The brothers are famously argumentative with each other.

A nondescript street in the
mass urban sprawl that is
São Paulo in Brazil is not easy
to find. The large, white roller
shutter offers no further clues,
but ring the bell and step
through the half-size door and
you enter the very individual
world of the Campana brothers.
Once the home of Fernando
Campana, it is now the centre
of the Campanas' ambition
to take the essence of modern
Brazil to the rest of the world.
This simple space filled with
the scent of burning incense
is home to their work and
their philosophy.

"Anything can be transformed from boring into fun."

Education Crasset studied at the Ateliers ENSCI, Paris. **Career** In 1991 Crasset participated in the Milan triennial, where she presented her project 'The Domestic Trilogy'. She then moved to Milan and worked with Denis Santachiara on various architecture and design projects. Returning to Paris, she started working with Philippe Starck and collaborated with him for five years. During this time she was also with Thomson Multimedia, where she became responsible for Tim Thom, Thomson's design centre. In 1998 she set up her own design studio and continued with a broad range of projects. In 2001 she began working on large-scale interior design. **Awards** In 1997 Crasset was awarded Le Grand prix du design de la ville de Paris. In 1998 the French Ministry of Culture granted her a FIACRE scholarship to develop her project 'Autogenous Design'. In 1999 she won Le Grand prix de la presse internationale de la critique du meuble contemporain. **Clients** Include Aquamass, Artemide, Authentics, Comité Colbert, Cristal Saint Louis, Danese, De Vecchi, D.I./M., Dolomite, Domeau & Pérès, Domodinamica, Dornbracht, Edra, Felice Rossi, Gandy Gallery in McDonough, Georgia, Grimaldi Forum, Hermès, Hi hotel, Nice, Lexon, Moeve, Orangina, PikaOne, Pitti Immagine, Première Vision, San Lorenzo, smak, Tefal, Tendence, Thomson Multimedia and Top Mouton. **Further information** Crasset is regularly invited to be a visiting lecturer at design schools in France and at the Danmarks designskole, Copenhagen, the Domus Academy, Milan, ECAL, Lausanne and the Gerrit Rietveld Academy, Amsterdam.

matali
crasset

"I am like other people. I eat three times a day. I sleep. I play with the children. I am also perhaps a workaholic."

A woman runs down the centre of a street in the Paris district of Belleville, as men sell their shoes at an impromptu street market. This is an area that is home to many immigrants, mainly Chinese. However, if you take a turning off the main street, go through a pair of giant green doors, a steel gate and along a perfect Parisian communal garden, you will find the highly colourful and playful home of Matali Crasset.

Opposite As one large, open space, the ground floor works as an office, a dining room, a sitting room and a kitchen. The brightly coloured squares were designed by Crasset and are used as multi-functional seating. Crasset also designed the table called 'Table, Tray, and Shelves', its name explaining its various possible uses. The chair at the end of the table is a 'Nextomechair' designed in 1999 by Crasset. The '4867' chairs either side of the table were designed by Joe Colombo in 1967. **Above left** The view from the spiral steel staircase looking down on to the ground floor. **Above right** Crasset's work space features a strong geometric shelving system, which she designed in one of her signature strong colours, and her 'Nextomechairs'. **Right** The industrial steel kitchen echoes the original structure of the building and acts as a screen in front of the spiral staircase.

10.

Education Day studied at the Royal College of Art in London from 1934 to 1937. **Career** His early work included sign writing, making drawings and models for architects as well as producing show cards for fashion boutiques. In 1947 he worked with the Architects Department of London County Council where he designed the seating for the Royal Festival Hall. In 1949 he was contracted to create his first furniture designs for Hille and became their Design Director in 1950. Day was a contributing designer to the Festival of Britain in 1951. In 1961 he was appointed as a consultant designer to BOAC (the British Overseas Airways Corporation) and designed aircraft interiors with his wife Lucienne Day. In 1963 he produced one of his most significant designs of the decade – the Polypropylene Chair, which is still in production today. He and Lucienne were design consultants for the John Lewis Partnership from 1962 until 1987. Throughout his career, Day has been commissioned to design public seating and furniture for clients such as British Rail, Gatwick Airport, Heathrow Airport, the Royal Theatre in Nottingham, the London Underground, as well as sports stadiums, arts centres and museums throughout the world. **Awards** Day's work has been widely recognized and awards have included the Low Cost Furniture Competition at the Museum of Modern Art in New York in 1948, a gold medal at the Milan Triennale in 1951 and British Design Centre awards in 1956, 1957, 1961, 1962, 1965 and 1966. In 1959 Day was appointed a Royal Designer for Industry. Robin and Lucienne Day received a Royal Society of Arts Design Management award in 1971 and joined the Royal Society of Arts design committee for the redevelopment of their headquarters in 1990. Day has also been awarded an honorary Order of the British Empire, is a SFRCA (Senior Fellow of the Royal College of Art), a FCSD (Fellow of the Chartered Society of Designers) and an Hon RIBA (Honorary Member of the Royal Institute of British Architects). **Clients** Include Hille, Heal's, Pye, Ekco, John Lewis Partnership, Magis and SCP. **Further information** Robin and Lucienne Day's contribution to post-war design has been charted in numerous books, articles and exhibitions including 'Hille: 75 years of British Furniture' at the Victoria and Albert Museum, London, in 1981, and 'Robin and Lucienne Day: Pioneers of Contemporary Design' at the Barbican Centre, London, in 2001. Robin Day is a keen walker and mountaineer. He lives with his wife, Lucienne Day, a prolific textile and wallpaper designer, in West Sussex, England.

robin
day

The sleepy county town of Chichester, West Sussex, is home to a cathedral and Robin Day. Day lives opposite the cathedral and talks passionately about its collection of work by artists such as Marc Chagall and Graham Sutherland. Now in his 90th year, Day is just as vital as ever. A vegetarian and a keen walker, he continues designing from the small wooden shed at the end of his garden. His clean-lined furniture fills the low-ceilinged cottage and looks as at home here as it would in any contemporary warehouse space.

"Maximum simplicity, calmness and quiet."

"I have learnt that intelligent and sensitive design can transform the quality of people's lives."

Opposite Maquettes for seating in Day's studio/shed. The one on the left is for his signature series of chairs designed for Hille and the one on the right is a unit for his recent 'Sussex' garden seating for the Italian company Magis. **Above left and above right** Day working at his drawing desk in his studio/shed at the end of his garden. The photograph on the wall behind him shows a panorama of the Alps; he has climbed many of the mountains.

11.

Education Gijs Bakker: trained in jewelry and industrial design at the Instituut voor Kunstnijverheidsonderwijs in Amsterdam from 1958 to 1962 and at the Industrial Design Department of Konstfack Skolan in Stockholm from 1962 to 1963. Renny Ramakers: studied art history and archaeology at the University of Leiden, graduating in 1983. **Career** Bakker was employed as a designer at Koninklijke Van Kempen & Begeer from 1964 to 1966. He became a freelance designer working for Polaroid, Castelijn, Artimeta, Artifort and Mellona among others. He lectured in the Design Department of the Academy of Fine Arts in Arnhemand from 1971 to 1978 and at the Delft University of Technology from 1985 to 1987. In 1987 he became a partner in BRS Premsela & Vonk Design Firm in Amsterdam and a professor in the Living Department of the Design Academy in Eindhoven. Ramakers was the design critic for the Dutch newspaper *De Volkskrant* from 1983 to 1987. From 1988 to 1993 she was the Chief Editor of the Dutch magazine *Industrieel Ontwerpen* and from 1993 to 1997 she was the Chief Editor of the Dutch magazine *Items*. From 1997 to 2000 she was the Managing Editor of a series of books on Dutch graphic design. **Awards** Bakker was awarded the Tweede Van Rijn Prijs for sculpture in 1965, the Prins Bernhard Fonds Prijs for Applied Arts and Architecture in 1995, the RA Award for jewelry in 1996 and the Françoise van den Bosch Prijs for jewelry in 1998. Droog Design has won several awards, including the Prix d'Excellence de la Maison and the Dedalus Award for European Design in 1998, the Cologne Thumper 2000 and the Kho Liang Ie Prize in 2000. **Clients** Include Rosenthal, Cacharel, Mandarina Duck, Flos, Oranienbaum, Salviati, Levi's, We and Picus. **Further information** Bakker co-founded 'Chi ha paura…?', a foundation for international jewelry design, in 1996. Ramakers is a member of several design boards and foundations. She has published articles on design in a number of international magazines and has written courses in design history for the Dutch Open University. Bakker and Ramakers have been lecturing at the Design Academy in Eindhoven since 2000. Droog Design have had solo exhibitions around the globe and have participated in more than 70 exhibitions worldwide. They have also produced a number of printed publications.

droog

Gijs Bakker lives in a picture postcard house by a bridge on one of Amsterdam's main canals. His desk overlooks the canal and the lounge at the back of the house overlooks a rural idyll of overrun gardens. Two worlds from one apartment linked by a marble hallway. Bakker loves Amsterdam.

Renny Ramakers lives a short walk away from her Droog partner, Bakker, in a converted school. At the very top of the building this vast open space is informed by the weather which fills every huge window. This is where she works and lives, with each area clearly defined by her choice of furniture style and colours. The colour orange and shiny surfaces are favourites. Ramakers likes to lie in the bath and look out over the Amsterdam rooftops.

"Low ceilings keep people dumb."

"Work, think, look, talk, eat, drink, enjoy, love, sleep…"

Opposite The sculptural garden trowel and fork are by Tony Gregg and were bought by Bakker at Tate Britain, London. **Right** A circular, white wall sculpture by Ad Dekkers. **Below right** Bakker restored the large, traditional marble fireplace; the circular occasional table in front of the sofa is by Achille Castiglioni and the sofa is by Vico Magistretti for Padova. **Below left** Bakker standing in the original marble hallway that links his working area overlooking a canal to his living space at the rear of the house; the chair is by Now I Miss The Picture.

Opposite A smaller, more intimate space off the main area retains the apartment's strong architectural theme. The chestnut leather sofa is an 18th-century piece. The glass and chrome trolley is from the 1930s. **Above left** The main living area is home to Ramakers's eclectic collection of furniture. The 'Arc' standard light was designed by Achille Castiglioni in 1962. **Above right** The 'Knotted Chair' was designed in 1996 by fellow Dutch designer Marcel Wanders.

Left The table-chair is by
Juergen Bey for Droog and is
one of their signature pieces.
Below left A classic 1930s
chair that Ramakers found and
re-covered in velvet. **Opposite**
Ramakers's favourite place is
the large bath which she sits in
and looks out over the rooftops
of Amsterdam.

"In the house and
the basic furniture
sobriety reigns,
in the objects it
is conceptuality."

12.

Education Gschwendtner was awarded a Masters in furniture design from the Royal College of Art, London, a furniture and product design degree from Kingston University, Surrey, and a Foundation Diploma in art and design from Central Saint Martins College of Art and Design, London. **Career** Since leaving the Royal College of Art in 1998, Gschwendtner has worked on everything from chairs to lights to egg cups. Establishing herself within the worlds of both industrial and exhibition design, she continues to work in both fields with equal success. **Clients** Include CTO, Innermost, Purves & Purves, Mathmos, Habitat, Twentytwentyone, WMF, Alma Home, Horm, Artificial, the British Council and the Victoria and Albert Museum, London. **Further information** Gschwendtner is a part-time tutor in contemporary furniture at Buckinghamshire Chilterns University College, England.

"Problem-concept-development-solution."

Gitta Gschwendtner lives on a wide North London street filled with imposing Edwardian houses. Hers is the one with the vivid pink front door. A fashion designer works in her lounge and Gschwendtner plugs her laptop in behind her bed. This is not a conventional home. She has a collection of electric irons and shops regularly in charity shops and at street markets, rarely spending more than 50 pence. Gschwendtner brings a love of colour, kitsch and the absurd to this grey corner of London.

Opposite The small wall-mounted bookcase is decorated with Christmas lights that Gschwendtner never took down and a donkey which is just one of her many charity shop finds. **Above right** A small part of Gschwendtner's collection of second-hand electric irons sits on the fitted wardrobes in her bedroom. **Above left** Gschwendtner in her junk shop armchair surrounded by her extensive collection of shoes and handbags. **Left** A corner of the bedroom with a 'Magazine Rug' and a 'Between the Lines' bedside table; both designed by Gschwendtner.

Opposite A collection of Gschwendtner's charity shop ceramic treasures. The wall colour was chosen by her and is referred to as 'sophisticated suffering'. **Above right** The lounge is very dark, small and filled with eclectic pieces all purchased cheaply. **Above left** The ornate seating in the lounge belongs to a friend of Gschwendtner. The painting on the wall is another charity shop find. **Left** A 'Basil Brush' light.

"We call the wall colour 'sophisticated suffering'."

Education From 1983 until 1985 Guixé studied interior design at the Elisava in Barcelona and from 1986 until 1987 he studied industrial design at the Scuola Politecnica di Milano in Milan. **Career** Having studied interior and industrial design in Barcelona and Milan, Guixé began working as a design advisor in Seoul, South Korea, and moved to Berlin. He started formulating a new means of understanding the culture of products and of exhibiting his work. His work strongly characterized his desire to search for new product systems, the introduction of design in food and the presentation of his creative ideas through performance. His non-conventional approach was soon noticed as he became internationally recognized for providing brilliant and simple ideas with a curious seriousness. After one of his exhibitions he was approached by the Mallorcean shoe company Camper and has designed forty of their shops worldwide and is responsible for their brand identity. He is now based in Barcelona and Berlin. **Awards** In 1985 Guixé was awarded the INFAD medal of interior design; in 1999, the Ciutat de Barcelona Design Prize; in 2003, 2nd prize for his graphic commercial posters for Marc Marti and 1st prize at Expohogar for his Plant-me pets and in 2004 he received the Design Plus award for his Plant-me pets at the Frankfurt Ambiente. **Clients** Include Authentics, Camper, Cha-cha, Chupa Chups, Desigual, Droog Design, Pure Lustre and Saporiti. **Further information** Guixé's work has been published in *Guixé 1:1* and the *Martí Guixé Cook Book*. His work has been widely exhibited.

marti
guixe

Opposite Guixé working in the main room in his apartment where doors lead on to two balconies which he does not use. The table and chair were both bought locally and cheaply. **Above top left** A detail of some of Guixé's works in progress. **Above top right** A collection of transparent storage boxes stacked in the apartment's main corridor. **Above bottom right** Guixé's diary/calendar/work to do wall. **Below top right** The bedroom has two single beds pushed together to form one large bed which fills the room. The 'Tizio' light on the floor in the corner was designed by Richard Sapper. **Below bottom left** Guixé's study is the smallest room in the apartment and is home to all his reference material and to his library. The 'Bobby' trolley in the foreground was designed by Joe Colombo. **Below left** The only decoration on the walls are two small images taped to the wall of his study by his girlfriend. **Below top left** The main room is home to a television and a collection of cheap buys and furniture found on the street. **Above bottom left** This Camper shoe box is the only reference to Guixé's main client.

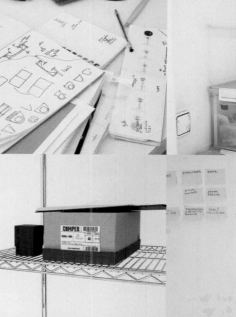

14.

Education Hecht studied industrial design at the Royal College of Art, London. **Career** On leaving the Royal College of Art, Hecht began working in the areas of architecture and design at the London studios of the architect David Chipperfield. He then started working internationally with the Studio Group and IDEO in San Francisco, Japan and London where he became head of industrial design. In 2002 he co-founded Industrial Facility with his wife Kim Colin. **Clients** Include NEC, Seiko Epson, National, Prada and Muji. **Further information** Hecht's first architectural work was the Watercycle Pavilion for Thames Water, London, and was completed in 2000. Industrial Facility's book *Things that Go Unseen* was published in 2003.

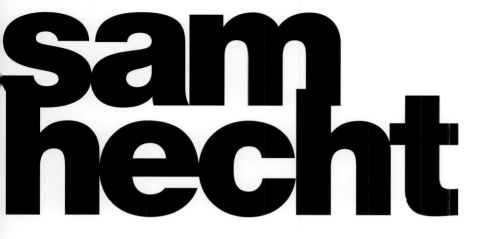

There is no knowing what lies behind the high brick wall in the extremely affluent area of St John's Wood, London. This house used to be a car repair shop and now it is a white box with a spiral staircase. Light pours in through the windows at the front, but there are none at the back. Wardrobes open and micro offices are inside, the hallway is the kitchen, and the best room in the house belongs to Hecht's four-year-old son. Hecht cycles across London to his office, buys toys for his son on e-Bay and has a pull-down projector screen to watch films on, but no television.

"Effort does not impress me – I prefer a lightness of touch."

15.

Education Hilton was awarded an Art Foundation Diploma, Portsmouth College of Art, Hampshire, England and a furniture and 3-D design degree from Kingston Polytechnic, Surrey, England. **Career** From 1980 to 1984 Hilton was employed as an industrial designer and model maker, designing and building detailed models of plastic-injection mouldings for casing electrical products. In 1984 he set up his own design studio and workshop designing and producing furniture in materials that ranged from aluminium to solid woods, through to upholstery and plastic-injection moulding. In 1997 Hilton was appointed as the Head of Furniture Design for Habitat UK, while continuing to work with other international companies through his own design office. In 2004 he left Habitat and began establishing a new design studio. **Awards** In 2000 he was awarded the *Homes & Gardens* magazine Classic Design Award (in association with the Victoria and Albert Museum, London). In 2003 he was nominated for the Compasso d'Oro for his 'Wait chair' and for the *Homes & Gardens* magazine Classic Design Award. In 2004 Hilton was appointed as a Royal Designer for Industry. **Clients** Include SCP Ltd, Driade, Disform, Sawaya, Moroni, XO, Montis, Perobell, Authentics, Handles and Fittings Ltd, Montina, Livit, Ycami, Andreu World and Habitat. **Further information** Hilton was a jury member for the 2000 International Furniture Design Competition in Valencia, Italy. He is a member of the selection panel 100% Design, London, and has been since 1996. His monograph, *Matthew Hilton: Furniture for Our Time*, was published to coincide with the eponymous exhibition at the Geffrye Museum, London, in 2000.

mat thew hilton

"I believe in quality."

There is a particular style of English architecture dating from the 1960s and 1970s that has yet to be truly understood – heavily influenced by European and Scandinavian thinking of the time, it is often ignored or, at best, underrated. Hilton lives in such a house in South-East London and is passionate about it.

Opposite A collection of found typography and garden implements creates a graphic still-life against the painted garden fence. **Right** A traditional blackboard diary rests on a chair in the kitchen and is regularly updated by Hilton.

"Design is just part of my life. I don't feel I have applied design principles to the house."

16.

Education Holtzman studied at the Park School, Baltimore, MD and undertook an intensive self-administered course in the decorative arts studying auction catalogues, with an emphasis on the early 18th century. **Career** Holtzman taught colour theory, two-dimensional design and stage design at the Villa Julie College, Maryland, before spending five years on one project, his own home in Baltimore. He created and installed every architectural and decorative detail himself, from doorknobs and cabinets to paint effects, furniture and textiles. When he was thirty-nine years old he sold his apartment and started *Nest* magazine with no publishing experience at all. He lives in New York and was the Editor-in-Chief and Art Director of *Nest*. He now pursues a number of related interests. **Awards** *Nest* magazine won numerous awards including seven of *Folio Magazine's* Ozzie Awards, Holtzman was the American Society of Magazine Editors' National Magazine Awards Winner in 2000 and a Cooper-Hewitt, Smithsonian National Design Museum's National Design Awards Nominee. **Further information** Holtzman has an extensive collection of the works of Christopher Dresser.

joseph
holtzm
an

"Design is what I do. Please don't think about that."

Nest magazine no longer exists, but its spirit lives on through its owner, editor and art director Joseph Holtzman. Originally trained as an artist and still fascinated by 'surface', Holtzman is never creatively content and is a self-confessed connoisseur. His approach, style and apartment are as unique as his magazine was.

Opposite A Donald Judd desk covered in carpet serves as Holtzman's working surface in his small foyer off the main living room. The Art Deco lamp base was designed by Oscar Bach who also contributed to the design of the iconic cap of New York's Chrysler Building. **Above left** Part of Holtzman's collection of what he calls 'jugs' which fill every space of the small foyer. **Above right** The shelving is by Jean Provet and was designed in the 1950s. Artist Patrick O'Brien painted the walls and the ceiling. **Right** Holtzman designed the wooden cabinets with a thousand perforations in his bedroom. The vintage Marcel Breuer chair with a cane seat has been made more comfortable with a pair of flea market cushions.

"Find things out for yourself. Ask questions."

Opposite A narrow, Japanese-style Herter Brothers bed created in the 1880s. The prints on the wall are by Richard Tuttle and are hung against photo tiles made from a repeated laminated image of some scrap cloth. The floor to ceiling shelving designed by Holtzman houses a small portion of his large fiction collection. The floor lamp by the bookcase is one of a pair that used to belong to Andy Warhol.
Below A collection of ceramics, sitting on a Louis XVI commode beside Holtzman's bed, which includes a pair of Sèvres pate sur pate vases commemorating the 1924 Paris Olympics.

17.

Education Mari attended the Brera Academy of Fine Arts in Milan in the early 1950s. **Career** He turned his attention to design in the late 1950s, fully aware of the need to work towards a global project of quality within mass culture and has continued to strive towards this goal ever since. **Awards** Mari's research work has won him approximately forty awards, including four Compasso d'Oro prizes in 1967, 1979, 1987 and 1999, as well as the Barcelona award in 1997. **Clients** Mari has created over 1,700 projects for clients such as Danese, Olivetti, Boringhieri, Adelphi, Driade, Le Creuset, Artemide, Castelli, Gabbianelli, the Municipality of Milan, Interflex, Zanotta, Fantini, Agape, Alessi, Zani & Zani, KPM, Robots, Ideal Standard, Arnolfo di Cambio and Muji. **Further information** His works have been exhibited widely throughout his career, including at the Venice Biennale, 1967, 1979 and 1986; at the Kassel exhibition, 1968; the 'Modelli del Reale' in the Republic of San Marino, 1988; the 'Arbeiten in Berlin', Berlin, 1996; 'Enzo Mari, Il Lavoro al Centro' in Barcelona, 1999; the Milan Triennale, 1999; and 'Tre Mostre di Enzo Mari' at the International Museum of Ceramics in Faenza, 2000. Examples of his art and design work can be found in many museums, including 9,000 drawings in the Archivio del Progetto of the University of Parma as well as the National Gallery of Modern Art in Rome, the Museum of Modern Art in New York and the Kunstmuseum in Düsseldorf. His teaching courses include those at the CSAC (the Centre of Archive Studies of Communication), University of Parma, the Academy of Fine Arts in Carrara, the Faculty of Architecture of the Politecnico di Milano, the ISIA in Florence and the Hochschule für angewandte Kunst in Vienna, Austria. His essay 'Progetto e Passione' was published in 2001.

Opposite Next to Mari's desk and work space are doors leading to the terrace – the feature that led him to purchase his apartment. The painting above the desk reads 'Il tutto è nulla' ('Everything is nothingness') in Japanese. The 'Filo di Ferro' desk is by Mari and was designed in 1991. **Below top left** The living room fireplace is used as a display stand for Mari's collection of found objects. **Below top right** An original fireplace is the focal point of the lounge area. The Glifo sectional shelving is used throughout the apartment to store just some of Mari's extensive book collection and was designed by him in 1967. He also designed the sofa. **Below bottom right** A bust entitled 'un frammento di statua da giardino' and boxed artworks by Mari. **Below bottom left** The Tojo floor standing light behind the sunflower is by Achille Castiglioni for Flos. The torso sculpture was made in 1951 by the Italian artist Fulvio Bianconi. **Overleaf left** A detail of the shelving next to Mari's desk. **Overleaf right** Mari seated on his terrace.

"To try to work and live in a way that is not alienating."

primavera del disseny
1997
design in Spring

Guardó Internacional Barcelona Disseny

atorgat a

Enzo Mari

per la seva destacada trajectòria professional,
per la seva reflexió crítica i per la seva aportació
intel·lectual en el camp del disseny.

Barcelona, abril 1997

El jurat: Ferran Amat, Mai Felip, Quim Larrea, John Thackara, Josep M. Tremoleda / Comissari

"Consumerism is based on the rapid obsolescence of each form."

"People tend to appreciate, the best you put before them."

A renovated industrial building, an hour's drive north of Sheffield, England, is home to David Mellor, his company and his factory. Surrounded by the rolling hills of Derbyshire, it is a retreat from the world of commerce, which allows Mellor to remain close to the base materials that have informed his entire career. He has always lived and worked near Sheffield, the home of British steel, and will never leave.

156

"A combination of functional efficiency and aesthetic appeal."

Opposite A glass corridor links the second-floor library with the main living area. The building is made of traditional local stone.
Above right The white painted wooden chair is by Hans Wegner and was restored by David's son Corin. The painting behind the chair is *Var Valley II* by Roger de Grey and the oil painting by Phillip Sutton above the log basket is entitled *Snape Landscape*. **Right** A low shelf made from beech runs along one side of the hallway and is used to display a Japanese metal bowl, three shagreen and silver boxes by John Cooper and a traditional doll by the craftsman Eric Horne. The large painting just in view is entitled *Homage to Sir Joshua Reynolds* and is by Paul Wyeth.

Left The steel staircase that leads from the ground-floor hallway to the first-floor living and kitchen area was designed by Mellor. The low table is by Corin Mellor and the painting, *Abstract*, is by Graham Bevan. **Below left** Part of Mellor's collection of traditional ceramics. **Below right** Looking across the lounge area. The handwoven rugs were made in Devon by Vanessa Robertson. The dark grey leather chairs are by Alvar Aalto, as are the low plywood stools. **Opposite** Mellor standing next to a traditional wood-burning stove in the lounge.

"Design better, buy less and recycle it."

In an area of South-East London filled with railway lines, junkyards and confusing road systems lives Jay Osgerby. His Victorian terraced house stands out with its simple grey door and lack of net curtains at the windows. Inside, the walls have been knocked through and the space defined by Barber Osgerby's trademark clean, simply constructed furniture and refined use of colour. Classic designs sit easily with junk shop finds and their own work. It all seems very natural. An oasis of modernism in a Victorian landscape.

Opposite The entire ground floor has been opened up and is used as a living, dining and kitchen area. The 'Elan' sofas were designed by Jasper Morrison for Cappellini, the 'Portsmouth' wooden bench is by Barber Osgerby for Isokon Plus, as is the 'Home' dining table. The chairs are by Arne Jacobsen for Fritz Hansen and the 'Loop Table' is by Barber Osgerby for Isokon Plus and Cappellini. **Clockwise, from top left** A wall calendar by Twentytwentyone. The 'Portsmouth' bench was originally designed by Barber Osgerby for Portsmouth Cathedral. One of a series of prints by Damien Hirst that he used in his Pharmacy restaurant in Notting Hill, London. Osgerby found the old haberdasher's wooden storage units in a local junk shop. The Harry Bertoia '420c' chair is by Knoll and was found at Portobello market in London. The table in the kitchen was manufactured by Ercol and the 'Flight' stools are by Barber Osgerby and were originally designed for a central London restaurant.

"The ground floor is one big room and the nicest space in the house."

Education Rams studied architecture and interior design at the School of Art in Wiesbaden, Germany, from 1947 to 1951. **Career** In 1953 Rams was employed by the architectural office of Otto Apel. He worked there for two years before joining Braun AG as an architect and interior designer in 1955. In 1961 he was appointed Head of the Braun Design Department, in 1968 he became Director of the Braun Design Department and in 1988 he was appointed Executive Director of Braun AG. He was finally promoted from the Design Department to become Executive Director of Corporate Identity Affairs at Braun AG in 1995, where he worked for a further two years before retiring to become Professor Emeritus of the Academy of Fine Arts in Hamburg. **Awards** Rams has won numerous awards, including the SIAD Medal of the Society of Industrial Artists and Designers in London in 1978. Haus Industrieform, Essen, named the Braun Design Department the 'Design Team of the Year' in 1989 and Rams was the first award winner of the Industrie Forum Design Hannover for his special contributions to design in 1990. He was awarded a World Design Medal from the Industrial Designers Society of America in 1996 and the Commander's Cross of the Order of Merit of the Federal Republic of Germany in 2002. **Clients** Include Braun, Gillette, Jafra, Otto Zapf and Vitsoe. **Further Information** Rams was made a member of the Supervisory Board of the German Design Council in 1976 and an honorary member of the Association of German Industrial Designers in 1977. He was Chairman of the German Design Council between 1988 and 1998, becoming an honorary member in 2002. In 1991 he became Doctor Honoris Causa at the Royal College of Arts, London. He was a board member of the International Council of Societies of Industrial Design from 1991 to 1995 and has been a regional advisor since. Rams has also been a member of the Academy of Arts, Berlin, since 1999. His work has been recognized through numerous exhibitions around the world. He is a keen gardener and swims everyday.

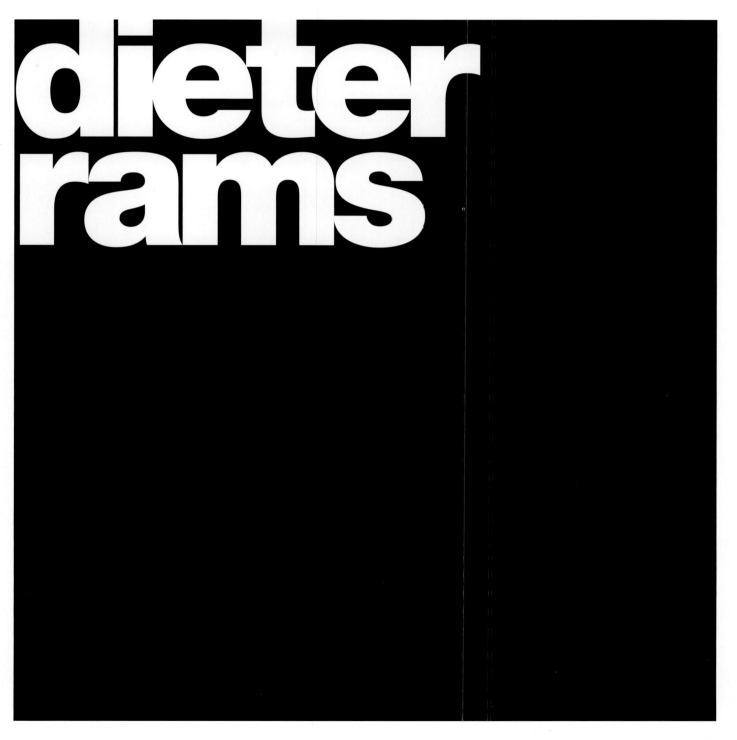

Above left Rams's large collection of reference books in his study are stacked on the 606 Universal Shelving designed by him for Vitsoe in 1960. **Above right** Rams's work space within the house opens on to the garden and the swimming pool. It is filled with prototypes and examples of his work. The table maquette in the foreground was made for a conference table. **Opposite** Rams on the upper terrace of the house he designed as part of a development for Braun workers.

Below The main entrance to the house. All the doors in the house are painted the same colour which Rams developed himself. The 'Conference stool 862' for Vitsoe on the left next to the kitchen was designed by Rams with Jurgen Greubel. **Opposite** These circular rugs are randomly placed on the ceramic tile floor that runs throughout the house and are used in all of the rooms.

"Eliminate the unimportant."

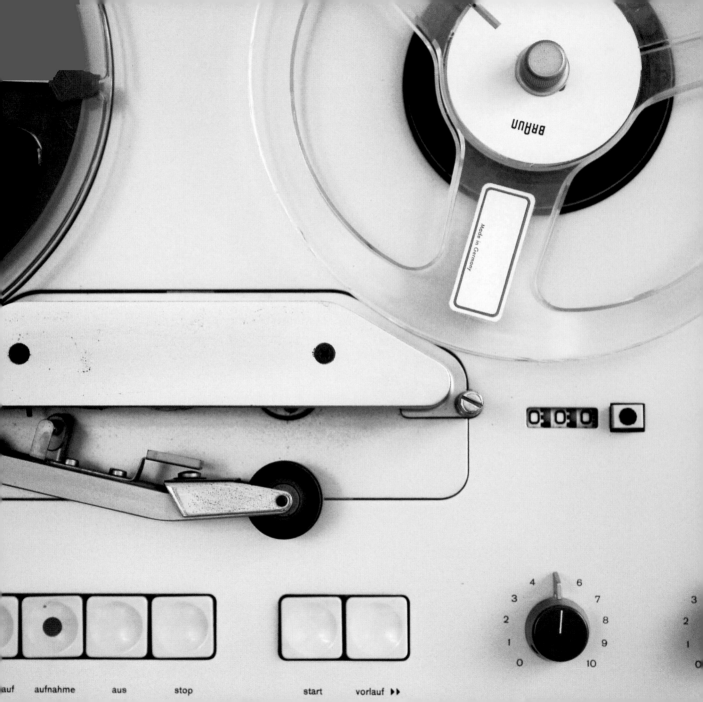

BRAUN

Made in Germany

auf   aufnahme   aus   stop   start   vorlauf ▶▶

Opposite A detail of a reel-to-reel tape machine, part of a Braun wall-mounted 'Audio 2/3 Hi-Fi' control unit designed by Rams (1961–63). **Left** Rams's spectacles on his office desk. **Below** A corner of Rams's work space where a carefully positioned selection of his designs shows his love of strong primary colours. The typewriter is by Olivetti.

21.

Education Rashid was awarded a Bachelor of industrial design in Canada. **Career** Rashid began working in Milan for Rodolfo Bonetto, before moving to KAN Industrial Design where he was employed for seven years. In 1993 he opened his own studio in New York where he works today. Rashid has designed and produced over 1,000 products during his career, so far. **Awards** Rashid has won numerous awards, including the Brooklyn Museum of Art Designer Award in 1998, the Daimler Chrysler Award, the George Nelson Design Award and the Philadelphia Museum of Art Collab Award in 1999, the Canadian Design Hero Award in 2001, *ID Magazine*'s Annual Design Review, Industrial Design Excellence Awards (IDEA), the International Interior Design Association Star Award in 2002, and *Bon Appetit's* Designer of the Year, *ID Magazine*'s Award for Design Distinction, Best of Category and Honorable Mention Awards, National Association of Store Fixture Manufacturers for Best Retail Store Design in 2003. **Clients** Include Prada, Issey Miyake, YSL, Umbra, Nambe, Magis, Edra, Frighetto, Herman Miller, Sony, Foscarini, Artemide, Idée, Bozart, Shiseido, Giorgio Armani, Leonardo, Nienkamper, Yahoo, Zerodisegno, Copco, Method, Guzzini and Danese, among others. **Further information** Rashid exhibits his art at the Sandra Gering Gallery and Deitch Projects in New York. He was a full-time Associate Professor in Industrial Design for ten years. He continues to write for various design publications and lectures frequently at universities and conferences around the world. A monograph on his work entitled *I Want to Change the World* was published in 2001. He also edited the *International Design Yearbook, 18*. Rashid is currently completing his second monograph entitled *Evolution*.

karim rashid

On a mid-town Manhattan cross street a nondescript white door opens on to a near vertical stairway at the top of which is Karim Rashid's apartment. Isolated from the sounds of New York street life during the day, all is quiet. It is a space that comes alive at night. This is planet Rashid. Rashid buys houses, cars and stereos on e-Bay, has an office downstairs and spends most of his time travelling. A truly international designer, his home in New York stays true to all he preaches.

"I want to be part of the entire world, working in every country, touching the souls of everyone."

punk Picasso

"I think today's fixtures are all so formal and part of that 'stylized tasteful bullshit.'"

Above left The 'Flexuous' wallpaper that covers one wall of the lounge was designed by Rashid for Wolf Gordon; on his desk are three of his 'Five Senses' vases. **Left** This is the view from the lounge through to the kitchen area, with a yellow 'Blob' floorlight by Rashid for Foscarini. **Opposite** Rashid's first-floor apartment consists of one large, open space. The lounging area is at the front of the building and is home to a collection of Rashid's designs as well as classic pieces that he has collected. The white 'Shroom' stool was designed by Rashid for Idee as was the black sofa; the pink swing chair was designed for Frighetto. The large painting is part of a triptych made by Rashid in 2002. The smaller framed artwork is by Christopher Wool, while the vintage white Bang and Olufsen stereo unit was purchased on e-Bay. The chess set in the foreground was designed for Bozart and sits on a 'Blob' coffee table; both are by Rashid.

186

"No preconceptions, no biases, no forced 'style' because 'styles' are the past."

Opposite A collection of Rashid's favourite pieces found on e-Bay including a doorstopper by Marc Newson. **Above right** The painting is by Rashid, as is the 'Metablob' stool and 'Alo' chair. **Right** Two pieces by Rashid: the 'Blob' white high table – despite all the colour in his work and apartment, white is his favourite colour to wear – and the 'Kovacs' floorlight lamp.

22.

Education Seymour studied at the Royal College of Art, London.
Career Seymour was an integral part of the 1980s street scene,
creating club flyers and, as a dj, playing hip hop, electro, dub
and ska in the underground club scene. In 1991 he was awarded
a scholarship to the Royal College of Art in London where he
developed his interest in design and sculpture. After graduating,
he travelled around the world, skating, snowboarding and
collaborating with other artists. In 1999 he opened a workshop
in Milan, where he began working on his own experimental
projects while collaborating with commercial clients. **Awards**
In 2000 he was awarded the Dedalus Award for European Design
and in 2000 and 2003 the Taro Okamoto Memorial Award for
Contemporary Art. **Clients** Include Magis, Nike, Kreo, IDEE,
Sputnik, Covo, Swatch, Perrier, L'Oreal and Smeg. **Further
information** Seymour lectures at the Domus Academy in Milan,
the Royal College of Art in London and the Vitra Design Workshops
in France. Exhibitions of his work include 'Bonnie + Clyde', the
Design Museum, London, 'Enter the Monkey', the Milan Furniture
Fair in 2002 and 'Lowlife', Galerie Kreo, Paris, 'Welcome to Scum
City', Gallery Facsimile, the Milan Furniture Fair, 'Tape', Palais
de Tokyo, Paris, and 'Welcome to Scum City Part II: Tokyo Style',
IDEE Tokyo in 2003 and 'Mo'Scum', Denim Gallery, New York,
in 2004.

jerszy seymour

An elegant Milanese courtyard is the unexpected entrance to the subterranean world of Jerszy Seymour. The raised ground floor is his girlfriend's space, the basement is Seymour's. Dominated by his moulded Ford Escort bedroom, everywhere you look there are statements of intent and works in progress. Everything in life seems to inform his designs and the two are inseparable in his home. He has an account with the café next door, where he and his collaborators often lunch and are supplied with a constant stream of strong coffee.

"The question for me is not 'what is design?', but 'why design?'"

ali tayar

23.

Education Tayar studied architecture at the University of Stuttgart and at MIT (the Massachusetts Institute of Technology) in the United States. **Career** After graduating, Tayar worked in the United States on wide-span hangar structures with Lev Zetlin Associates, on tensile structures with FTL and on curtain-wall design with James Carpenter. In 1993 he formed the Parallel Design Partnership through which he designs and produces furniture and hardware. **Awards** Tayar was awarded a design grant in 1995 from the National Endowment for the Arts and two *ID Magazine* Design Distinction Awards in 1994 and 1999. **Clients** ICF Group and Magis. **Further information** Tayar's previous projects include the following in New York: the Gansevoort Gallery, the Waterloo Brasserie, the Midway Restaurant, the PoP lounge and the John Frieda Salon on Madison Avenue. A collection of furniture pieces designed for the ICF Group was presented at the International Contemporary Furniture Fair in May 1999 and an injection-moulded shelving system for the Magis Company was developed in 2002. Parallel Design's award-winning aluminium shelving system, 'ellen's brackets', is widely available and is featured in Aveda shops across the United States. Tayar recently completed a loft in the Richard Meier Tower, New York. Ongoing projects include a retreat on Block Island, a house in Cape Town, South Africa, and the Glass/House in Southampton, New York State.

The meatpacking district of Lower Manhattan is fast becoming home to upmarket fashion shops, hotels and restaurants. It is also home to Ali Tayar's workspace/apartment in a renovated print works. He has lived and worked here for twelve years and has seen changes that seem to him to occur on an hourly basis. He claims not to be able to afford to buy an apartment anywhere else in Manhattan, but his connection with the space and the area may be the real reason he stays.

"The most important thing is to keep working on new stuff. The last man standing will win."

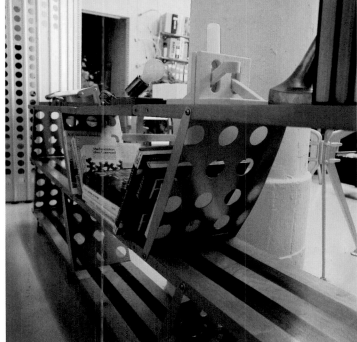

Opposite A 'Raymonds' armchair designed by Tayar and covered in 'Clarence House' fabric. On the low table, also designed by Tayar, is a photograph of his father. **Above left** The 'Rasamny Bench' in the foreground was designed by Tayar as was the 'Michaels' dining table. Tayar bought the chairs for $50 at a second-hand shop twelve years ago to furnish his first office. The 'Plaza' aluminium screen that divides the main space was designed by Tayar in two parts. **Above right** Detail of an 'Elephant' table designed by Tayar on which rests a glass case containing a scale model of Tayar's first major architectural project, a retreat for an academic couple on Block Island. **Right** The 'Anna' shelving is home to design prototypes.

Terence Woodgate lives in
a converted school sanatorium
with its own wood and three
acres of land in the East Sussex
countryside. With his children's
skateboards scattered around
the entrance hall, home-made
chutneys in the kitchen and
a wood-burning fire in the
living room, this is very much
a family home.

"I endeavour to create things that age well, that mellow and even improve with age."

Opposite The view from the large entrance hall into the living area. The chair upholstered in orange wool was designed by Woodgate for Montina. He also designed the table which was made by cabinet maker Charles Thompson. The painting on the left is part of a group of four encaustics by Grant Watson and the one on the right is *Shadow No. 38* by Brad Lochore. **Above left** A vase and bowl by Poole Studio Potteries. **Above right** Next to the living room fireplace are a grain hut ladder from Mali and a grain bowl from Chad.

"I do consider myself very lucky to love my work."

Right Two Poole Studio Potteries vases and a sculptural piece by Lee Critchlow are displayed on white shelving designed by Woodgate specifically for the living room. **Below** The minimalist children's bathroom. **Opposite** The entrance hall opens on to a large eating area and kitchen. The kitchen units were designed by Woodgate in a midnight blue. The painting is by Woodgate. **Overleaf** Three of Woodgate's Punt Mobles home storage units that lead from the entrance hall past the children's bedrooms to their bathroom. A collection of African musical instruments are displayed on top of the units. Suspended against the end wall is a gong from Indonesia.

alberto alessi

Where do you live?
Actually, at the moment I'm homeless!

A few years ago I left my first home, which I called 'La Casa della Felicità'. It was designed in the 1980s by some of my most beloved architects of that period: Bob Venturi, Aldo Rossi, Ettore Sottsass, Achille Castiglioni, Riccardo Dalisi and Milton Graves, under the direction of Alessandro Mendini. It was in Omegna, northern Italy, on Lake Orta and was very beautiful and functional.

For the last three years I have been in the process of designing my new home, again with the help of Alessandro Mendini. It will be in an old farm, in the hills of Lake Orta, with a breathtaking view of the island of San Giulio. It's a big farm of about 50,000 sq m and will be completely renovated, but will retain its original spirit.

How long have you lived there?
I plan to live there in a few years.

What was the starting point for its design?
Calm, simplicity and maximum luxury.

Which room do you feel is most successful?
The library and the kitchen, I hope, as in my former home.

How have your design principles influenced your home?
Very strictly…for example, at the moment I feel the need for calm and simplicity, as I have said, and also luxury, both in design and in architecture.

What is design?
Design is a new form of art and poetry and very typical of our times. It's a kind of global creative discipline with an artistic and poetical matrix.

How have your views on design changed since you began your career?
They have not really changed. Since the beginning I have felt the same. Of course, what has changed are the ways to give body to my vision and the form that design has taken in different periods.

What have you learnt?
I've learnt that there is a fight, in human beings, between technology and poetry. But it's a nice challenge, I mean poetry vs technology like David vs Goliath.

Who are your heroes?
Mmmm…let's say mainly architects. I consider the maestros to be people such as Bob Venturi, Ettore Sottsass, Richard Sapper, Achille Castiglioni, Alessandro Mendini. And from industry I'd like to mention Walter Rathenau of AEG.

Where do you seek inspiration?
Almost exclusively by thinking and by listening to other people thinking.

How do you begin working on a project?
My preferred way is to answer a telephone call from one of the hundreds of designers I'm working with, saying to me: 'Alberto, I've a wonderful idea for you'.

What do you prefer to work with? Computer? Pencil? Pen?
Computer.

How do you reconcile design with consumerism?
I'm not sure there is a way to do so. Well, sometimes I feel there is a way. The history of applied arts has been a long journey into man's history, a journey during which real progress has always been sought by exploring the territory located between the possible and the real, between daytime and nighttime. This journey

is expected to last much longer yet and I believe industry has to play a key role in it. I can clearly see that society's progress will consistently stem from a continuous interaction between business and culture. But, beware, I am not referring to the so-called culture of mass production, to that 'industrial culturalism'. To put it in Baudrillard's words, that 'which we insist on calling culture in spite of all misunderstandings, to that strange substance made up of messages, texts, images, bestsellers or comic strips, to that codified creativity which has replaced inspiration and sensitivity.' Quoting Baudrillard again, and in part contradicting him, I am referring to culture and my work in an attempt to work 'even in the hyperfunctionalism of a wasted culture, with a view to universality, to the transcendence of myths which might decode our age without being mythological super-productions thereof, to an Art able to decipher our modernity without dissolving in it.'

What is the one thing that every home needs?
Beauty.

What could you not live without?
Beauty.

What kind of environment do you like working in?
Chaos + memories + always new things to keep me awake.

How does it differ from your living space?
There is no difference.

Describe an average day.
**7.30: wake up and eat breakfast with Laura and little Emma
8.30: office, mail and meetings
13.00–15.00: back in my office for mail and messages from my collaborators (I confess that sometimes I personally need to write the instructions on how to use my new objects!)
15.00–19.00: working on projects in development, finding new ideas, etc.**

What is important?
Nothing, except details.

What are we getting right today?
It depends on how I wake up.

Nature or nurture?
Talent and passion, those are the two gifts needed to handle good design. Then, of course, talent has also to be nurtured and passion has to be controlled.

Should a home be 'a machine for living in'?
Yes, but a poetical machine.

What is taste?
Taste is our own metre, our personal way to measure the distance from human beings and God, from immanence to transcendence.

What's your favourite material to work with?
All kinds of metals.

How do you feel you've made your mark?
Passion, sensibility and intuition.

If you were asked to give the world a single piece of advice, what would it be?
Listen very carefully to your demon.

What will the house of the future look like?
Like the home I'm designing with Alessandro Mendini: it will be beautiful, calm, have a big library, a good kitchen, an enormous table for everything and a comfortable bed.

What's next?
To find the way to balance peace and excitement.

harry allen

Where do you live?
My partner John and I have an apartment in the East Village of New York City and a house in Bedford, New York State.

How did you find your home?
I bought the building.

How long have you lived there?
Six years.

What was the starting point for its design?
I started out living in the apartment alone and at that point I was concerned with only a few things. I wanted a really functional kitchen in which to cook, a large dining table to seat all my friends, a large sitting area to retire to after dining, a place to sleep and a place to bathe. For every project I employ my design sensibility, but I also try to make sure I reflect my client. In this case I am applying my design principles to my life. Much of the art in the apartment was given to me by friends

and family. I have designed or collected much of the furniture. Most importantly, it is alive, it changes almost daily, we re-hang the art, we get new things, we get rid of the old, we re-arrange, we try things out. That is the fun of it all.

Which room do you feel is most successful?
The main room, which incorporates a dining and living area, is the most striking. The apartment was created with friends and entertaining in mind: an industrial kitchen, a table that seats twenty and a couch that fits equally as many.

How have your design principles influenced your home?
It works both ways. My design principles influence my home and my home influences my design principles. Necessity is the mother of invention after all. For instance, the renovation process was

an exercise in reduction. It is all about carving out a rational space. As far as decoration, I am a collector really. I like to use my designs, but I also like art, design history and just beautiful objects. I believe that if you assemble a group of beautiful, interesting things all together they will become a beautiful, decorative scheme and will speak of the inhabitant, the collector. I don't really subscribe to the whole pattern and colour-matching system of interior design.

What is design?
I look at it as imposing rational order.

How have your views on design changed since you began your career?
I have matured. Life stepped in and taught me a few lessons. In the beginning I was working in a vacuum and I created some very good stuff there, but I have been exposed to a great

variety of people, projects and places. You can't just walk in and apply this very rigid perspective. You have to learn, adapt and experiment. Through that process your perspective changes – you find new creative ground. You keep all the criteria you started with and just keep on adding to that. It gets harder to satisfy all the criteria, but when you do you get really great designs.

What have you learnt?
People want things that work. People want comfort. People like wood and warmth, familiar materials. You don't have to re-invent the wheel every time you do a project. One must leave tolerances – what works on paper does not always work in real life. Everything should be level and square before you start work.

Who are your heroes?
I've got a very broad base of interest and I don't

always look to design and designers for inspiration. As an American designer, I must acknowledge Ray and Charles Eames. And I love the work of George Nelson and Henry Dreyfuss. Contemporary designers would be difficult, but would definitely include Konstantin Grcic, Jasper Morrison and Ali Tayar. Architects would include Tadao Ando and Rem Koolhaas.

Where do you seek inspiration?
Art, History, Nature, Engineering and Travel.

How do you begin working on a project?
I listen. I observe. I think. I sketch. And usually there is a flash of inspiration, the first thought about a project, which should always be honoured and pursued.

What do you prefer to work with? Computer? Pencil? Pen?
All of the above. I really only sketch these days and I am not very particular about the medium. My amazing staff then take it and make it look real, either via hand renderings or the computer. And all the technical drawings are done on the computer.

How do you reconcile design with consumerism?
Design is meant to be sold, or to sell. It is a marriage of art and industry, or culture and commerce. There is no need to reconcile design with consumerism, because in its nature design is commercial.

What is the one thing that every home needs?
Thought.

What could you not live without?
No family? No food? No soap? Unqualified, this is a scary question, but I will concentrate on material goods. Perhaps it is my bed. It is king size, but since this is an exercise in reduction, I could manage on a queen. I'd love a Dux, but I will settle for a Sealy.

What kind of environment do you like working in?
I like light and organization. I currently work in a completely open space, but it could really use some division.

How does it differ from your living space?
Only functionally. Home is about eating, sleeping and bathing. Work is about work. Aesthetically there is not much of a difference in philosophy.

Describe an average day.
Every day is so very different – and I like it that way. I am a pretty early riser – 6 to 7 am, maybe a bit later if I can afford it or I have been out the night before. Breakfast and newspaper with my boyfriend John. Commute one and a half hours from the country/ one minute in the city, work work work, lunch, work work work. Stop at about 5 or 6. Dinner with friends or at home, or a movie. But really, there is no average day.

What is important?
I was just in Frankfurt for the housewares show and it really made me want to puke. All that crap, so much of it, people buy it and we burn up the world to make it. I really want my life

to be filled with love, culture, good food and drink, friends and family, nature, exercise, thought, music and a few good things. I aspire to collect the best things, not many, but just a few of the best and to make the rest.

What are we getting right today?
In respect of design I think some examples of companies that are getting it right are Prada, Aveda, Apple and many of the fashion brands. Even mass-market retailers, like Target, are making great design available to everyone. However, I think the US lags behind in areas of design and design education. Having said that, I like the ecological consciousness that permeates the design community; I like the art-based, conceptual direction of design; I like the humble, functional aesthetics that continue to be developed in many areas of design. Experimentation with new materials and methods, such as digital media and robotics, are things that we are getting right today with a view to more conscious quality living.

Nature or nurture?
Nature.

Should a home be 'a machine for living in'?
If you think about it every home is really a machine in that it serves some function, it serves our lives.

What is taste?
Education.

What's your favourite material to work with?
Whatever I am working with

at the moment. There are only potential favourites.

How do you feel you've made your mark?
I like to think that I will take a place in design history – just a few more ideas that mark an era and maybe move culture forward a bit. I hope I have inspired a few younger designers to push the envelope even further. I think my early materials work was pretty important; at least it has been collected and is in a few museums. But I have so much more to design so it might not yet be time to be talking about my mark. Doesn't that all get sorted out after you die?

If you were asked to give the world a single piece of advice, what would it be?
Take down your Christmas lights after New Year's Eve. No, really, it would be to conserve energy, resources and just conserve in general.

What will the house of the future look like?
I am by nature drawn to rational architecture. It seems that designers and architects are just so happy that they finally have a tool that enables them to build anything, that they build anything. With the maturation of computers people stopped thinking about what was appropriate. I think all this blobitecture and amorphous form is a bit ridiculous, like the cars of the fifties. I do not like design that screams 'look at me'.

What's next?
For me, reality. I have been making products whose forms are cast directly from life.

azumis

Where do you live?
Hackney, East London, in a disused toy factory which has been converted into a live/work unit.

How did you find your home?
By visiting every type of house and apartment in London, before finding that this open-space type was the most suitable for us – a studio and a home under one roof.

What was the starting point for its design?
Maximizing its functionality and separating the office and the private space.

Which room do you feel is most successful?
The dining area – with its soft light through the steel-framed door and windows, and off-cut wooden panels as a back drop to where we eat and get together.

How have your design principles influenced your home?
Our way of design is reflected in our home; it is functional and everything has a reason to be there – but it is not too dry.

What is design?
A means to a purpose, with a grace to its existence.

How have your views on design changed since you began your career?
We began observing everything – space, objects and how people react to an environment.

What have you learnt?
Too much to describe – we learn from our everyday life, travel and meeting people. From everything.

Who are your heroes?
We are influenced by many objects, the environment and pieces created by known and anonymous people – it is difficult to pick just a few.

Where do you seek inspiration?
Anywhere.

How do you begin working on a project?
It depends on the type of project. Normally, we discuss what could be the horizon that we can push further.

What do you prefer to work with? Computer? Pencil? Pen?
We use bits of everything in several stages of the work process. We like to use them all.

How do you reconcile design with consumerism?
If a product is well designed and good quality, it lasts longer.

What is the one thing that every home needs?
Harmony.

What could you not live without?
A comfortable bath.

What kind of environment do you like working in?
Bright, open, ordered and functional.

How does it differ from your living space?
There is no difference.

Describe an average day.
There is no average day, every day is different. One day, we work all day at our studio, in front of the computer. Another day, we are abroad meeting with our clients, visiting factories and eating local food.

What are we getting right today?
Healthy food.

Nature or nurture?
You have to be grown up.

Should a home be 'a machine for living in'?
The machine has to provide not only physical functionality, but also psychological functionality.

What is taste?
A personal matter.

What's your favourite material to work with?
We always try to choose the most appropriate material within the context of the work.

How do you feel you've made your mark?
Although all our work is united by a way of thinking, we tend not to make 'our mark' on each design.

What will the house of the future look like?
Not much different.

What's next?
We do not know...

yves behar

Where do you live?
San Francisco (Oakland to be precise), California.

How did you find your home?
We found each other…she was a mess, I was one too…there was some fixing to do…

How long have you lived there?
Six years.

What was the starting point for its design?
A good basic structure in the middle of the north California landscape…just like the Golden Gate Bridge which we can see from the house.

Which room do you feel is most successful?
The living room, with its fluid dialogue between inside and outside, as well as the fluid transition between the kitchen, dining and living rooms. One detail seems also to work well, the soft undulating floor-tile transition between the shower and the bathroom.

How have your design principles influenced your home?
Keeping the transitions fluid and natural, with wit and sensuality.

What is design?
Putting ideas into a form that can be emotionally and visually experienced.

How have your views on design changed since you began your career?
From a purely modernist functional education in Switzerland, to a less dogmatic and more emotionally centred approach. Reaching people with ideas through my work is always the motivation. The fuseproject motto became: 'design brings stories to life'. The important element here is that design can speak ideas and communicate.

What have you learnt?
That the practice of design has become about content: smart and witty. It is not about style and establishing a visual signature. Design is a personal endeavour pursued as a means of communication. Ideas are what I try to communicate in my work, and every project is about forming a point of view, from which ideas can be expressed and stories told.

Who are your heroes?
Achille Castiglioni, Antoine de Saint Exupéry, Hussein Chalayan, Isamu Noguchi, Tintin…

Where do you seek inspiration?
I seek inspiration in the extraordinary and the ordinary. The ordinary being the texture of everyday life, personal wit and dissatisfaction with the way things are. The extraordinary being nature, new dreamed technologies, human sensations and human emotions.

How do you begin working on a project?
**I tend to develop a point of view derived not from my own aspirations, but from three main outside sources of inspiration:
1 the conditions surrounding the project
2 the client's own history and untold story
3 the intelligence of the public the project is intended for.**

What do you prefer to work with? Computer? Pencil? Pen?
All of the above. A pen when writing ideas, a pencil when creating the first sketches, and computers when finalizing a project.

How do you reconcile design with consumerism?
Design that creates a pause from blind consumerism is what I look for, design that offers a thought or a

reflection, design that makes one smile or makes one feel human.

What is the one thing that every home needs?
A fireplace and a door to a green area.

What could you not live without?
A connection with the ground and being close to where gravity is pulling us. As well as the knowledge that a house is a meeting point, where friends and family gather for a shared experience.

What kind of environment do you like working in?
An open environment, without walls, where information and ideas flow freely.

How does it differ from your living space, if at all?
It does not, the living space attempts to 'open' rather than 'close'.

Describe an average day.
The first look is for a view of nature and the bay. The second look is to my laptop (unfortunately). After a short drive, the third look is for designing and reviewing. The rest of the day is a game of listening and making.

What is important?
To participate, to give, to love and to feel alive inside.

What are we getting right today?
What is right is the human emotion, but we also get it wrong every day by suppressing it.

Nature or nurture?
Understand nature, nurture with encouragement and respect.

Should a home be 'a machine for living in'?
Not a machine when it comes to the current definition of the word. In the near future, though, home technology will become like second nature. A self-sustaining organism that lives 'with us' rather than 'for us'.

What is taste?
The confidence to create an identity out of your personal background and vision.

What's your favourite material to work with?
I don't really have a favourite material, I love a full toolbox of varied and unusual materials.

How do you feel you've made your mark?
By designing from the 'inside-out'…creating a curiosity out of the mundane category of commercial products and by mixing traditional gestures with the futuristic. Not designing the same thing twice.

If you were asked to give the world a single piece of advice, what would it be?
Look inside before looking outside.

What will the house of the future look like?
It will be incredibly technological, sensing, automated…and at the same time highly personalized, customized and individual.

What's next?
A swim in the ocean.

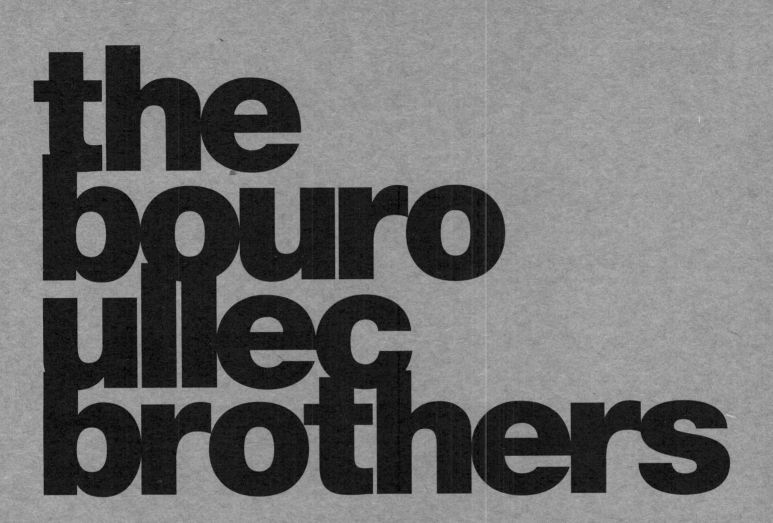

the bouroullec brothers

Where do you live?
At present we live the life of gypsies and have nowhere to live. We work in a fifty-year-old workshop, which is something between a house and a warehouse, lost in an anonymous street, in a northern suburb of Paris.

How did you find your home?
We were looking for a space to base the studio and an incredible phone battle secured it.

What was the starting point for its design?
To isolate it, and then paint everything white.

Which room do you feel is most successful?
Well it's an open space, and has no rooms.

How have your design principles influenced your home?
To keep it as much as possible structurally undefined. That means
not building any new walls and creating the different places throughout with furniture.

What is design?
Our borders are that definition. Creating elements that have a function, and which are aimed to be reproduced.

How have your views on design changed since you began your career?
It depends, but the foundation of design is for us a question of context. I would say that our views evolve in reaction to each project.

What have you learnt?
To communicate.

Who are your heroes?
Anyone acting strangely in a situation with a lot of humour.

Where do you seek inspiration?
We keep our eyes wide open, which means we can find it in art, such as the cinema or in novels, but as our work is focused on creating everyday objects, we also look at someone sitting on a tree trunk, or an old man lighting his pipe.

How do you begin working on a project?
A ping-pong game, each of us on one side of the table, with paper and pencils.

What do you prefer to work with? Computer? Pencil? Pen?
Work is on the one hand deeply intellectual – it means a step-by-step construction in which you have and remove, then modify something that will then be born. On the other hand, pens, computers, cardboard, tape, or a restaurant napkin are a way to fix ideas and help their evolution within our thought process.

How do you reconcile design with consumerism?
We respect the many diverse ways of producing an object. Of course a plastic chair is cheap and affordable for most of us, and then an incredible hand-blown glass bottle from Murano is something rarer. Who can tell which is the most reasonable product? We consider that they both have to live together. The objects that surround us create an incredible jungle of different ways of making things and from our point of view, it should remain like this.

What is the one thing that every home needs?
We would say a door handle, but it's not suitable for many places we've been. Then we imagine a table, but we have eaten on the floor – maybe a tap, but it could be a bucket, then…maybe an ashtray.

What could you not live without?
Perhaps a cigarette lighter.

What kind of environment do you like working in?
The most incredible spaces we have ever worked in have been the unexpected large tables, discovered in unexpected places, sometimes with the snow falling outside, or a fresh breeze coming through the window… It can happen when you're travelling and you find a deserted restaurant, or a sun terrace on a mountain… Of course, this can never be deliberate, but only expected and never repeated.

Describe an average day.
Waking up too late, going to bed too late.

What is important?
To listen.

What are we getting right today?
We step into the jungle, or the future whichever you prefer.

Nature or nurture?
A zen garden.

Should a home be 'a machine for living in'?
That would mean that we would become some kind of train driver. A home has to be a place that grows

with you and a tool that you need to make work for you. The home could be seen as a large table, where you can settle many different activities, but also a single vase and a coffee cup.

What is taste?
Taste is what you assume as a personal decision, without any doubt about it.

What's your favourite material to work with?
We don't have any favourite material. It is usually a choice driven more by the question we have to answer.

How do you feel you've made your mark?
By doing things to our own taste.

If you were asked to give the world a single piece of advice, what would it be?
We really don't know, but personally we'd better stop smoking.

What will the house of the future look like?
Again, we really don't know, but personally we'd like to buy another warehouse to live in.

What's next?
The next question.

boym

Where do you live?
CB: We live in New York on the Lower East Side, one of the oldest areas of Manhattan, which has been the home for countless immigrants, mostly Jewish and Italian, since the early 19th century. In the 1960s, the programs of 'urban renewal' ruined the character of the area – the neighbourhood fell out of fashion and was considered unsafe. Many New Yorkers simply never used to go there.

How did you find your home?
CB: After the birth of our son eight years ago we could not continue living in our small Greenwich Village apartment. At that time the Lower East Side was one of the 'last frontiers' in Manhattan, still unaffected by the real estate frenzy. We were amazed to discover The Amalgamated House, an architectural gem built in 1929 as a co-op for garment workers. In the 1920s, the co-operative movement was a kind of radical social group aimed at liberating the workers from the slums and giving them freedom and a better life. To that end, they provided spacious apartments with tree-shaded courtyards, fountains and elaborate arched gateways. This is our home now.

How long have you lived there?
CB: Over seven years.

What was the starting point for its design?
CB: My first desire was, of course, to start knocking down walls here and there, opening the space – a typical ex-architect syndrome. Fortunately, financial and structural constraints prevented most of this destruction. It took a while to understand the meaning and beauty in the existing layout of the apartment, and to find a way to express and re-contextualize the spaces in a more subtle way.

Which room do you feel is most successful?
CB: I like the rooms with the pale-coloured vignettes – it is as if they were stage sets or memories of other imaginary apartments. All the furniture we use is either designed by us, by our friends, or is from the companies we have worked with. A chair is not just a good-looking chair; it also has a memory associated with it. These personal memories add to the look of the space, and make it 'more than meets the eye'.
LL: We like to have fun with the environment and the room themes often change. I decided on 'hedonism' for the bedroom. It gave us a chance to display my collection of J. H. Lynch dusky maiden prints from the 1960s. There is a lingerie-pink alcove where they are displayed and low blond furniture pieces juxtaposed against a few 'high design' Droog Design pieces.

How have your design principles influenced your home?
**CB: I do not subscribe to the oft-expressed designer's wish, 'I want to change the world'. My idea is rather to play and experiment with the things we have already, to try to see them with a fresh eye, to place them in a new, unexpected context. And this is, essentially, what the design of the apartment is about. It is perhaps less 'wild' than some of our other projects, but this is very much intentional. The purpose here is not to provoke or amaze someone, but to live here.
LL: Our house really reflects our individual personalities. I subscribe very much to the high/low dichotomy:** carefully considered objects placed next to each other can enhance the understanding of the objects, or create a new meaning for them. I dress that way, listen to music that way, so naturally our place should reflect that sensibility.

What is design?
CB: In the widest possible sense, design is a universal activity of creating and arranging material things. To do your own home is designing, and every human being partakes in this activity, at one time or another.

How have your views on design changed since you begun your career?
CB: In our book *Curious Boym* I called for designers to look at the monkey Curious George, a children's book character, as a role model. The role of the designer today is to be continually on the look out – to detect all the intangible vibes of emerging needs, trends and desires, and, then, as Tom Ford used to put it, 'try to give people what they want before they know they want it'. This is the way our studio works.

I started on experimental, self-generated projects. Now we at the studio are more interested in applying the same principles to our projects for clients.
LL: I've become more accepting of who Constantin and I are and how we can contribute in our own way to the profession. Being a young designer is about being full of idealism, or a fantasy of what you can do. Over time, you learn to develop a sense of where you belong on the continuum… Actually some designers never figure that one out.

What have you learnt?
CB: That this is a lifetime job.

Who are your heroes?
CB: Andrea Branzi, who taught me that design is first and foremost a conceptual activity. The late Tibor Kalman, who, in spite of being very successful, managed to keep that critical subversive edge in his work and Murray Moss in New York, who single-handedly raised the bar for American design a few notches, both in a visual and an intellectual sense.
LL: Also, Paola Antonelli, curator of Contemporary Design at the Museum of Modern Art in New York, one of the most beautiful people in the business with an enormous heart.

Where do you seek inspiration?
CB: Our projects reflect on everyday aspects of American lifestyle and landscape, on familiar things that often pass unnoticed because of their very proximity.

LL: I've always been very interested in subculture and marginal fields. There are commonalities between filmmaking and the design process, or fashion and furniture for that matter. I like to exploit these similarities in our studio work.

How do you begin working on a project?
CB: I approach every project as a conceptual challenge, so at first it is all about thinking, not sketching. Often, I get a first and definitive design idea while riding a subway, or flying in an aeroplane.

What do you prefer to work with? Computer? Pencil? Pen?
CB: We use the most appropriate means – these days it is mostly the computer.

How do you reconcile design with consumerism?
CB: I do not see a conflict. People in developed countries are completely saturated with good, functional things. What they need are objects that speak to their emotions, their collectors' instinct and their need for communication. This is a need and, of course, there is great consumerism hiding there as well.

What is the one thing that every home needs?
CB: An object of desire, a thing that makes the owner proud and satisfied.

What could you not live without?
LL: Soy milk and an alarm clock are essential to the inner mechanics of my household.

What kind of environment do you like working in?
CB: At this point, we like to have as little 'stuff' in the studio as possible. For years, we have worked in a workshop-like environment which got cluttered with objects, materials and machines. Now, we consider the studio as more of a laboratory of ideas rather than a shop, and the lab has to be clean.

How does it differ from your living space, if at all?
LL: Our living space is cleaner than the office, and both are cleaner than our 19th-century farmhouse near Woodstock, New York.

What is important?
LL: Good energy is more important than anything. Without it nothing gets done.

What are we getting right today?
LL: An ability to develop our chosen profession, have a profitable business and wonderful clients. Our son is an honour student at the top public school in Manhattan. So, there is a lot right in the Boyms' house today.

Nature or nurture?
LL: Nobody can accomplish anything in this life in a vacuum. I've always been lucky enough to have people with great energy around me, so it's all about nurture.

Should a home be 'a machine for living in'?
CB: Le Corbusier himself has added in his writings that the machine for living 'must emotionally move me'.

What is taste?
CB: I have too often been accused of not having it… Ultimately, taste is a social convention and many unconventional things are almost automatically being referred to as 'tasteless'.

How do you feel you've made your mark?
LL: By bringing humour to design. I can define a similar sensibility in creative people in adjacent creative fields, but I believe it's our significant contribution to design.

If you were asked to give the world a single piece of advice, what would it be?
CB: Be curious.
LL: Just ask for it!

What will the house of the future look like?
CB: I think it will be a relatively free space, with a lot of techno-gadgets and functional furnishings hidden and built in, with quite a few non-functional emotional objects – souvenirs, collections, heirlooms – proudly displayed on the outside.

What's next?
CB: The next project.
LL: Dinner.

piero busnelli

Where do you live?
Anzano del Parco, in the province of Como, an hour north of Milan.

How did you find your home?
It is not exactly the home where I live. It is the result of a restoration, inside a park covering an area of 160,000 sq m and belongs to the local council. This is where I display my hunting trophies, cases and cabinets for collections and objects of particular sentimental value. There are tables that can be joined together when large groups of friends come for lunch, or separated and used as roomy work surfaces for browsing the many albums filled with my travel photos. The house in the park represents a sort of retreat, where I can find the peace life no longer allows, where I can relax, recalling the past.

How long have you lived there?
Seven years.

What was the starting point for its design?
The intention was first to create a sort of 'display area' for my hunting trophies, a place we jokingly referred to as a 'mausoleum'. I was interested in the architecture, of course, but from the earliest sketches I wanted to create a space where I could gather objects that are important to me. I visit on a daily basis and I am constantly devising new solutions for the landscaping of the park. However, unlike in the past, today, I really prefer my animals alive!

Which room do you feel is most successful?
The heart of the house is without doubt the living room.

How have your design principles influenced your home?
I have no ideas or principles that have radically influenced my home: I love comfort and I absolutely don't want to become a slave to design. There is, however, an element that influenced my choices, light. I love well-lit rooms and wide windows.

What is design?
I think it is difficult to find one definition of design, although it has never lost its original meaning as a project-based activity applied to industrial products. The interpretation of the word is extremely subjective. Design means being able to understand your own living conditions and to create a situation that can satisfy your needs.

What have you learnt?
I have to mention the development of cold-foamed polyurethane as applied to the furniture market, which I personally found out about and introduced to B&B Italia in 1966. Today, it represents one of a series of achievements that has made the company a success. I have also learnt to co-operate with designers, to understand how complicated the development of a project is and how many phases precede the realization of the finished product. The choice of designers and the selection of the products play the main roles. It is important to be able to understand and consider the customer's needs, finding the right balance between the company's strengths and the designers' creative ability in order to conceive products never influenced by the vagaries of fashion.

Who are your heroes?
Afra and Tobia Scarpa, the architects whom I started this exciting adventure with and who have designed some of the most successful of B&B Italia's pieces.

Where do you seek inspiration?
From the polyurethane technology I have mentioned.

How do you begin working on a project?
This project was a particular challenge…it was somewhat disheartening to witness the decay of the place. The building was largely in ruins and did not seem to bear any relation to the surrounding landscape, apart from the two magnificent plane trees at the entrance.

What do you prefer to work with? Computer? Pencil? Pen?
I don't like working with a personal computer, or with a pen. I prefer observing, thinking, working out ideas and working directly on the product.

How do you reconcile design with consumerism?
Finding a meeting point between design and consumerism represents the key to success for any company. B&B Italia was originally started with the intention of making low-price products and satisfying customers' needs, but then the importance of research, design and innovation as competitive factors and strategic elements in the company's development policy forced this to change. Today, B&B Italia is a leading company in the world of high-class contemporary furniture. It has therefore found is own balance within the high-end market with high-quality products and a high-design content.

What is the one thing that every home needs?
It's difficult to think of only one thing…but it is extremely important, in my opinion to, 'have plates within reach'.

What could you not live without?
An ambience that fully satisfies your own living needs. Things have to be in the right place, so that you can use everything easily.

What kind of environment do you like working in?
After many years devoted to work, I now prefer spending my time with people that I care about a lot, I dedicate myself to things that I like.

How does it differ from your living space, if at all?
At weekends I usually go to Liguria to enjoy my new, important project, a 32-foot boat that I have named PAB (Piero Ambrogio Busnelli). I keep it at the Lavagna dockyard.

Describe an average day.
Although I continue visiting the company daily, during the week I love spending my time in the park or at home, in my living room, having a look at the newspaper, reading a book or watching TV.

What is important?
I often think about where we are heading – the direction in which the world is going. The more I think, the more I cannot find a justification or an explanation for the violence and numerous wars killing so many innocents every day.

What are we getting right today?
Nowadays most young people are unsure, not responsible, not mature and I am worried to think that in the future the world will be in their hands.

Nature or nurture?
Both. The suitable solution is always to find the right balance.

Should a home be 'a machine for living in'?
I am not an enthusiast about the definition of the home as 'a machine for living in'. The home should be conceived as an ambience made to measure for the people who live in it. I believe that the housewife, or whoever lives in the house most, should make the choices.

What is taste?
Taste is to be able to place objects and furniture so that everything works perfectly.

What's your favourite material to work with?
It must be polyurethane.

How do you feel you've made your mark?
I believe I 'have done something' in my life, something important, with B&B Italia and it has created so many collections that represent the history of Italian design today.

If you were asked to give the world a single piece of advice, what would it be?
I will give two pieces of advice. First, be tolerant towards yourself and other people and, no less important, try and make our children responsible.

Nowadays young people grow up too fast, in a world that doesn't make our choices easier and that affects their behaviour. The schools take their part in the child's growth, but the parents' involvement is essential.

What will the house of the future look like?
The 'house of the future' doesn't exist. The architect has to be able to project in order to consider and emphasize the owners' lifestyle.

What's next?
Unlike what has happened in the past, society can now influence our furniture choices towards different styles. Thanks to communication we have a faster diffusion of ideas and an increase in people's level of design consciousness. The wide choice of furnishings has to be intelligently considered. What is important is to make careful choices based on quality and good taste that respond either to emotional needs or lifestyle expectations suggested by the domestic lifestyle.

the campana brothers

Where do you live?
São Paulo, Brazil.

How did you find your home?
Through a friend of ours who was buying this old loft which had previously been used by a transport company.

How long have you lived there?
Twelve years.

What was the starting point for its design?
First of all to divide the loft into two areas with a space in the middle which brought light into the new areas.

Which room do you feel is most successful?
The top floor.

How have your design principles influenced your home?
It is our laboratory where we apply our ideas.

What is design?
Design is functionality plus emotion.

How have your views on design changed since you began your career?
By being more observant and open to our everyday environment, as well as that of others.

What have you learnt?
To be humble.

Who are your heroes?
**Fernando: Birds.
Humberto: None.**

Where do you seek inspiration?
Where we think it exists.

How do you begin working on a project?
By creating a real-scale prototype.

What do you prefer to work with? Computer? Pencil? Pen?
To go straight to the real-scale model or use a BIC and a piece of paper.

How do you reconcile design with consumerism?
As with any other kind of exaggeration – it is not useful.

What is the one thing that every home needs?
A bed.

What could you not live without?
Fernando: Music.
Humberto: Sex.

What kind of environment do you like working in?
Peaceful.

How does it differ from your living space?
No distinction, except for the noise outside my window.

Describe an average day.
Fernando: Boring.
Humberto: Anything can be transformed from boring into fun.

What is important?
To laugh.

What are we getting right today?
Recycling.

Nature or nurture?
Nature.

Should a home be 'a machine for living in'?
It depends on the inhabitant's personality and mood.

What is taste?
Something that you can't buy.

What's your favourite material to work with?
There is no distinction for us once we are attracted to a material which can be recycled.

How do you feel you've made your mark?
This is too pretentious to think about at this point in our career.

If you were asked to give the world a single piece of advice, what would it be?
Stop fighting (in all senses).

What will the house of the future look like?
Never ending.

What's next?
Next.

matali crasset

Where do you live?
In the Belleville area of Paris. It's a very popular melting pot of a district, with people from China, North Africa, Turkey…all living together. We live a hundred metres from a unique building designed by Oscar Niemeyer and Les Buttes Chaumont, the garden created by Napoléon III.

How did you find your home?
My husband found it and it's where we live and work. We were looking for a studio, but we couldn't find anything which wasn't too small or too expensive. After looking at about fifty properties, we found it and decided to buy it within ten minutes. I really like to live and work in the same place, it's a real luxury because I am near my children and I can see them even if I'm working.

How long have you lived there?
Five years.

What was the starting point for its design?
As we have four different floors, the goal was to keep it as open as possible. There are only four doors in the whole house, no walls and no curtains mean that we are able to keep the maximum daylight. Even in the toilet, there is a transparent ceiling to let the light in.

Which room do you feel is most successful?
The space we live in the most is the first floor, because it's connected to the yard through a small garden. It's where we eat outside with our neighbours and where the children play. We like this space, but we like the relationship we have with our neighbours even more.

How have your design principles influenced your home?
There is no piece of furniture more than one metre in height and all the furniture is flexible so that we can easily create empty spaces if necessary.

What is design?
For me it's an experiment based on relationship and space.

Who are your heroes?
No master, no slave.

Where do you seek inspiration?
In everyday life.

What do you prefer to work with? Computer? Pencil? Pen?
With my head. A computer, pencil or pen is only an extension of what I think and a way to communicate with people.

What is the one thing that every home needs?
Life.

What could you not live without?
Neighbours.

What kind of environment do you like working in?
My home/studio.

How does it differ from your living space, if at all?
Not at all.

Describe an average day.
I am like other people. I eat three times a day. I sleep. I play with the children. I am also perhaps a workaholic.

What is important?
Friends.

Should a home be 'a machine for living in'?
A machine to play.

What is taste?
My husband's cooking.

What's your favourite material to work with?
No material. Concepts always come first.

If you were asked to give the world a single piece of advice, what would it be?
Be free.

What's next?
Projects are in the pipeline, but ask my clients – I have no idea of what the future will be. They have better dreams than me. I don't dream of designing a hotel or a pigeon loft. The only thing I try to do is to be free and open-minded.

robin day

Where do you live?
Chichester, West Sussex.

How did you find your home?
Through estate agents.

How long have you lived there?
Five and a half years.

What was the starting point for its design?
It was built some time in the 17th century. Then four years ago we installed our stuff from our home of forty-seven years in Chelsea, London.

Which room do you feel is most successful?
The office.

How have your design principles influenced your home?
Simplicity, calmness and comfort, giving us a relaxed 'lived in' home.

What is design?
Design is a small word with many meanings. For this book, I suggest its meaning is to give order and form to the environment and to all artefacts including architecture.

How have your views on design changed since you began your career?
They haven't, except I have realized that design can also be dangerous in promoting a lot of trivial rubbish which is not needed.

What have you learnt?
I have learnt that intelligent and sensitive design can transform the quality of people's lives. It can also be a mere expression of designers' egotism and the growth of consumerism.

Who are your heroes?
Design heroes? Charles Eames, Hans Wegner and the many anonymous designers who have developed things such as bicycles, umbrellas and many other items of brilliant, functional equipment.

Where do you seek inspiration?
Everywhere.

How do you begin working on a project?
Sometimes a brief by a client, or more often when I have what seems a worthwhile idea.

What do you prefer to work with? Computer? Pencil? Pen?
Pencil and pen – very much hands on. I make models, sometimes prototypes and do full-size working drawings. I am not a computer or drawing board stylist.

How do you reconcile design with consumerism?
By trying to design for real needs.

What is the one thing that every home needs?
Space.

What could you not live without?
My family.

What kind of environment do you like working in?
Maximum simplicity, calmness and quiet.

How does it differ from your living space?
It is more austere.

Describe an average day.
In my 90th year, a little work, some walking, reading, enjoying meals.

What are we getting right today?
Hopefully, we are slowly becoming aware that humanity is destroying our planet and some moves to check this are underway. Design has a place in this endeavour. Design to endure, conserve materials and energy, and avoid obsolescence.

Nature or nurture?
Nature.

Should a home be 'a machine for living in'?
Yes, but a lot more besides. It should give joy and visual and tactile pleasure.

What is taste?
Intelligent design.

What's your favourite material to work with?
Timber, metal, plastic. As a vegetarian I now worry about leather and skins.

How do you feel you've made your mark?
Perhaps by designing things which for over half a century are still made, bought and enjoyed, which hopefully means they are not merely fashionable.

If you were asked to give the world a single piece of advice, what would it be?
It would be arrogant to answer this question.

What will the house of the future look like?
Hopefully, environmentally friendly.

What's next?
Anybody's guess.

Gijs Bakker
Where do you live?
In the centre of Amsterdam.

How did you find your home?
**The famous Dutch designer
Benno Premsela was living
here in 1993 when I sold my
former home in Amersfoort
and wanted to buy a house
with a studio in Amsterdam.
During a meeting with
Benno, who was also a
great friend, I told him,
desperately, that I couldn't
find anything – it was all
too expensive. He simply
answered, 'why don't you
buy my house?' So I did.**

How long have you lived there?
You know now!!!!!

What was the starting point for
its design?
**There was no need for
design, it was perfect when
I moved in.**

Which room do you feel is most
successful?
**I love them all, the studio
with a view of the canal and
the sitting room with a view
over the garden.**

How have your design principles
influenced your home?
**Totally, some say it looks
like a warehouse, others
say it's like a museum.**

What is design?
**Observing objects,
observing people using
objects. Designing is
putting question marks.**

How have your views on design
changed since you began your
career?
**My view has never changed,
it has grown.**

What have you learnt?
**In the beginning I knew
nothing, in school they
taught me nothing,
everything I have learnt
in life has been through
my creative work.**

Who are your heroes?
**Alexander Calder, Bruno
Munari, Enzo Mari.**

Where do you seek inspiration?
**I isolate myself on my Dutch
island (5 x 60 m).**

How do you begin working on
a project?
**I read (not about design),
I empty myself, I try to
become a curious child.**

What do you prefer to work
with? Computer? Pencil? Pen?
Brains.

How do you reconcile design
with consumerism?
I am a consumer.

What is the one thing that every
home needs?
**A high ceiling, low ceilings
keep people dumb.**

What could you not live
without?
Music, new compositions.

What kind of environment do
you like working in?
Clean and organized.

How does it differ from your
living space?
It's all the same.

Describe an average day.
**I wake up at 7 am, have
my coffee and toast and
exercise. At 9 am I answer
my emails at home and at
10 am I do the same at the
Droog Design office. I work
until 9 pm and, if I am lucky,
I then go home to cook my
own meal. Unfortunately, I
am usually out for meetings
over dinner.**

What is important?
Concentration.

What are we getting right
today?
**My day is great when I have
no appointments and when
I am alone!!!!!!! It happens
seldom, alas.**

Nature or nurture?
Nature.

Should a home be 'a machine
for living in'?
**Good heavens, no! I am not
a machine and nor is my
home.**

What is taste?
**Individual choice, which
has nothing to do with good
or bad taste. I hate a house
that is stuffed with design
and contains no sign of the
individual.**

What's your favourite material
to work with?
Material follows concept.

How do you feel you've made
your mark?
**Form follows concept, the
form is only the wrapping of
the idea. This is my way of
working.**

If you were asked to give the
world a single piece of advice,
what would it be?
Keep religion out of politics.

What will the house of the
future look like?
**I don't think in the future,
I live and think in the now.**

What's next?
**Tomorrow, I am going
sailing and I won't look
at my diary for two days.**

Renny Ramakers
Where do you live?
In a loft in the centre of Amsterdam.

How did you find your home?
Through good luck, friends living in this wonderful house were going to move.

How long have you lived there?
For six years.

What was the starting point for its design?
Light, air, space and comfort.

Which room do you feel is most successful?
The bathroom.

How have your design principles influenced your home?
Not my design principles as such, but my personal needs: a functional environment for the various things I possess and use. In the house and the basic furniture sobriety reigns, in the objects it is conceptuality. Both sobriety and conceptuality are the cornerstone of Droog Design.

What is design?
There are numerous definitions of design. For me, it is simply creating the products we use and this can be done in a proper and an improper way.

How have your views on design changed since you began your career?
During my career, design has become more and more a matter of style and appearance which has increased my interest in sobriety and conceptuality.

What have you learnt?
Too much to write down.

Who are your heroes?
Nelson Mandela, Achille Castiglioni, Rem Koolhaas.

Where do you seek inspiration?
In the world around me.

How do you begin working on a project?
With a flow of thoughts.

What do you prefer to work with? Computer? Pencil? Pen?
I am not a designer, but a design critic/art historian so this question does not apply to me.

How do you reconcile design with consumerism?
Why should I?

What is the one thing that every home needs?
A bed.

What could you not live without?
The sun.

What kind of environment do you like working in?
Any environment, as long as I can open the windows and it has enough room for the space I like to work and live in.

How does it differ from your living space?
The difference is, above all, a matter of colour. In my living and working space at home white and sandy colours rule. In my working space at Droog I am surrounded by numerous shades of green.

Describe an average day.
Work, think, look, talk, eat, drink, enjoy, love, sleep...

What is important?
An open mind.

What are we getting right today?
In general, not too much.

Nature or nurture?
Both.

Should a home be 'a machine for living in'?
One should consider this statement by Le Corbusier in the time and context in which it was written. Le Corbusier and his contemporaries were inspired by the aesthetics of mechanization. Functionality can also work with non-machine-like aesthetics.

What is taste?
There is only dispute about taste.

What's your favourite material to work with?
The computer.

How do you feel you've made your mark?
With a worldwide positive response from people I respect.

If you were asked to give the world a single piece of advice, what would it be?
Open your mind.

What will the house of the future look like?
Thank God we don't know.

What's next?
Thank God we don't know.

gitta gschwendtner

Where do you live?
Finsbury Park, London.

How did you find your home?
An ad in Loot, a free newspaper.

How long have you lived there?
Eight and a half years.

What was the starting point for its design?
It's a rented flat so it was a case of doing the most with what was here with minimal effort and resources.

Which room do you feel is most successful?
I like the living room quite a lot. The idea was to make a room lacking in daylight work by painting it dark since it was never going to be a bright room. At night it looks lush and cosy, but it's a bit too dark during the day. We call the wall colour 'sophisticated suffering'… I am not sure whether this qualifies as successful.

How have your design principles influenced your home?
I tend to have narratives at the heart of my designs and I guess there is a bit of story-telling going on in my home, too.

What is design?
Problem-concept-development-solution.

How have your views on design changed since you began your career?
I guess they have not changed that dramatically. My career only spans six years and I still have the same outlook as I had then. In a career way I am less impatient and naive now, but my beliefs remain.

What have you learnt?
Stick to what you believe.

Who are your heroes?
My heroes are inspirational people.

Where do you seek inspiration?
Everyday life, art, travel, cinema, design…

How do you begin working on a project?
By brainstorming and writing lists and briefs and then rewriting them.

What do you prefer to work with? Computer? Pencil? Pen?
I work with all three.

How do you reconcile design with consumerism?
Since I am positioned in a relatively uncommercial market I am not that concerned with consumerism. That said, the connection sometimes frightens me, naively, since I have never really seen design as a tool to industrialize the object, but as pure creativity.

What is the one thing that every home needs?
A roof.

What could you not live without?
A roof, but once that's provided I would hate to live without a bath.

What kind of environment do you like working in?
My studio, preferably when it's busy with other people working and chatting away.

How does it differ from your living space?
It's an open-plan warehouse (in the most unglamorous way) with five work places, a workshop and a leaking roof. My flat is in a terraced house with a garden.

Describe an average day.
There is not really such a thing as an average day. The morning is the most average – I have breakfast in the bath and then make my way to the studio. Once there I check the mail and messages and look at what the day has to offer. From then on it really depends on what I am working on. It could be design, admin, a meeting or research.

What is important?
Balance.

What are we getting right today?
Sometimes we get the balance right, but often we don't.

Nature or nurture?
Both.

Should a home be 'a machine for living in'?
No, a home should be a place of comfort and compromise. Imperfection is as valuable as functionality.

What is taste?
Subjective.

What's your favourite material to work with?
Ideas.

How do you feel you've made your mark?
With persistence, if at all.

If you were asked to give the world a single piece of advice, what would it be?
That's quite a big question. I am not sure how to answer this without sounding like Miss World.

What will the house of the future look like?
Probably like the house of the past, but hopefully more environmentally friendly.

What's next?
Hopefully, progress.

marti guixe

Where do you live?
I live in an apartment in Barcelona a third of the time, an apartment in Berlin another third and the rest of the time I have to travel.

How did you find your home?
My father gave it to me fifteen years ago. He lives outside Barcelona, in the countryside.

How long have you lived there?
On and off for fifteen years, but during that time I have also lived in Milan and Berlin.

What was the starting point for its design?
The starting point is that it is not designed, I just did some basic work, bought basic furniture elements and even took some from the street.

Which room do you feel is most successful?
I am not so happy at home, home is only a transitory space. I am happy in the bar under my apartment, or in my friend Paco's restaurant, or walking to the city centre. The room I use most is the one where I have my big screen to which I connect my laptop. This is the place where I communicate for work.

How have your design principles influenced your home?
In the way that there is nothing purely for representation, only function. I don't like to possess objects, but I need to use them, so the whole is reduced to basic and useful elements.

What is design?
To design is to manage the complexity of a project in order to produce a desired result. This result can be of any shape or material and the only condition is that it should not be spontaneous or a product of an accident. Well, it could be like that, but only if it is part of the plan or project.

How have your views on design changed since you began your career?
As society has become more complex, I have begun to manage and to understand this complexity. When I studied design there were no personal computers, no mobile phones and the world was divided into two big blocks. Now everything has changed, so it is obvious that my views and approach have changed and are still changing, as I am trying to be contemporary and live in a contemporary way.

What have you learnt?
That nothing is permanent and that the value of products and things is based on the possibility of change and adapting to the continuous changes of society and a consumerist society.

Who are your heroes?
I have no heroes.

Where do you seek inspiration?
I don't believe in inspiration. I work by acquiring, having and processing information, and taking logical, coherent, reasonable decisions depending on the goals of the project in relation to its context.

How do you begin working on a project?
By communicating with the client and building a context for the project.

What do you prefer to work with? Computer? Pencil? Pen?
I only work digitally; everything is done with the digital tablet, keyboard and all kinds of software.

How do you reconcile design with consumerism?
Design is part of consumerism.

What is the one thing that every home needs?
An Internet connection.

What could you not live
without?
**Ice cubes, I buy them at the
petrol station.**

What kind of environment do
you like working in?
**Any working software
interface.**

How does it differ from your
living space?
**I have Windows on my
laptop! It doesn't differ.**

Describe an average day.
**In Barcelona, I wake up,
I have breakfast in the bar
beneath the apartment.
I communicate and work on
my computer. Sometimes
I visit someone for private
or professional purposes.
I go for tapas locally.
I communicate and work on
my computer. Sometimes
I meet a friend or attend
an exhibition. I go for tapas,
depending on the day, in
some pre-defined locations.
I go to sleep.**

What is important?
**To not have many things,
to be less tied down and
flexible, and movable.
Matter is against
contemporary lifestyle.**

Nature or nurture?
Culture.

Should a home be 'a machine
for living in'?
**No, the concept of 'a home
for living' is completely
conservative – you live in
each place you are or you
go. What does 'living in'
mean – does it mean that
you only live if you have a
conventional space where
you accumulate emotional
objects with no function in
order to build yourself a
protective and illusory
cocoon to be more secure**

**in your personality? Or
does it mean a context for
building family codes and
extending the existence
of the human psyche?
I understand a home as
a geographical address (in
a few years even that will
not be necessary) and a
place for body maintenance,
sleeping and personal
hygiene, including
physiological maintenance,
in other words, privacy.**

What is taste?
A sense.

What's your favourite material
to work with?
Information.

How do you feel you've made
your mark?
**By being radically effective
and contemporary.**

If you were asked to give the
world a single piece of advice,
what would it be?
Use Very Lustre.

What will the house of the
future look like?
Like mine.

What's next?
**Well, I am not interested
in what is next, just in what
is now.**

sam hecht

Where do you live?
London.

How did you find your home?
It took a while to find, even though I walked past it almost every week.

How long have you lived there?
Three years.

What was the starting point for its design?
The house is modern and small, no more than 1200 sq ft, but split into three floors. This effectively means one room per floor – one function per floor. So the idea was to create some kind of continuity, a way of living that is seamless, rather than the common prescription that each room requires its own character. We spent a long time using the landscape of the site (its orientation, its material) to influence how each wall or window acted. Every detail has a reason for its existence.

Which room do you feel is most successful?
Our son's room – its flexibility allows many characters to be played out. It's a room I would want as a child.

How have your design principles influenced your home?
I didn't look for the house; it came to me. Part of it was built in 1930 and in this sense, modernity from that time and modern ideas now are a very different species. But I wanted them both to live side by side. It's an odd house for London – modernism in England is always thought of as the territory of social housing, rather than privately commissioned housing. In Los Angeles, where I spend time every year, it's the direct opposite.

What is design?
When I know, I'll tell you.

How have your views on design changed since you began your career?
I've been lucky enough to collaborate with some brilliant people and I think my views have not changed, but grown broader. I think one area of my work has changed, though, quite noticeably and that is my approach to technology. The domestication of technology is the most uncharted water for design and there is so much to learn and respond to.

What have you learnt?
That design is transcendental rather than calculated.

Who are your heroes?
Shiro Kuramata and Jacques Tati. They continue to offer me so many secrets.

Where do you seek inspiration?
Riding my bike. Call me mad, but I have conversations (I don't know who with) when I ride. It also happens when I clean. I love to clean because it allows me to hear voices and have extraordinary conversations that wouldn't happen otherwise. Some people take a lot of drugs to have this opportunity! But for me it's cleaning…and travel. Travel is something I've done for most of my adult life. I find travelling the most potent form of creativity. If you're thinking 'do I clean when I travel?', the answer is no! I couldn't handle that amount of inspiration.

How do you begin working on a project?
Often with the most rational clarity imaginable. This way the essential starts to make itself visible and this is what all clients deserve. We do an enormous amount of research for each project, often without the client realizing. I have no time for mediocrity, so it's important for me to understand all of

the issues. I don't regard myself as a problem solver (by solving a problem you often create another), but more as an editor.

What do you prefer to work with? Computer? Pencil? Pen?
All of the above, sometimes at the same time. Making models is the crucial starting point – reappraising, questioning… it must work in totality.

How do you reconcile design with consumerism?
The world is always in constant change – we will always require new things whether they are thoughts, objects or landscapes. Design should give sense to these, by creating familiarity, while also suggesting possibilities. Dumb consumerism is the start point and the end point is the shop, and this is not design.

What is the one thing that every home needs?
Space (and a sponge!).

What could you not live without?
Space.

What kind of environment do you like working in?
I like experimentation, which by nature involves mess and confusion.

How does it differ from your living space?
I try to avoid mess and confusion where I live.

Describe an average day.
I get up, I go to the studio, I talk with people, I have a good lunch, I work some more, I go home, I play with the children, I have some
dinner, I talk some more, I go to sleep – all are important to me.

What is important?
Effort does not impress me – I prefer a lightness of touch. There is no need to see, feel or hear effort, in the hope of appreciation. For instance, humour that is dry and spontaneous is so much more successful than the planned joke.

What are we getting right today?
More conflict exists today than at any other time, so in a macro view I am not sure we're getting much right. But in a micro view, I cherish the freedom I have to live and work across so many borders. This is something we are getting right and long may it continue and grow.

Nature or nurture?
A combination. Humanity has significant power that is beyond genetic predisposition.

Should a home be 'a machine for living in'?
Only if it is a home built for the person inhabiting it. Inheriting someone else's machine can often be a hindrance.

What is taste?
When more than one person appreciates something, it could be implied that it is of good taste. But when it becomes populist, taste converts to fashion. I tend not to concern myself with fashionable desires – oddity is so much more interesting and risky. If you don't take a risk, the only route is to copy…

What's your favourite material to work with?
I always think of material as part of an idea; its connotations are absolute to me. So I use the appropriate material for the appropriate job, with its test being in specifics. I think every good designer does this.

How do you feel you've made your mark?
I let others decide this.

If you were asked to give the world a single piece of advice, what would it be?
Avoid all prejudice.

What will the house of the future look like?
A Barratt home of course. Sadly, little can change this on-going scenario until the government forces construction companies to involve progressive architectural ideas. Until that happens, the best ideas will continue to live as concepts.

What's next?
An advanced light system that is powered by human energy.

matthew hilton

Where do you live?
In a house built in 1967 in a cul-de-sac – it is one of a group of thirty-two houses in South-East London designed by the architect Peter Moiret. They are surrounded by space, trees, birds and foxes, rare in London. They have very well-designed internal spaces, with a feeling of light, air and a feeling of community which was obviously a consideration for the architect.

How did you find your home?
I was exploring the area one evening and noticed the houses. I liked them immediately and put a note through all the doors asking if anyone was selling and I was lucky.

How long have you lived there?
Four years.

What was the starting point for its design?
We haven't changed the interior much. We did take a wall out downstairs to make the kitchen bigger and we've decorated, but that's all – it's pretty much as it was when we bought it. The colours we chose are fairly neutral and the house has a relaxed, quiet feel about it. The success of the house is due to the quality of the architecture, not our interior design. We have just tried to respect the initial concept and bring out the best aspects of it.

Which room do you feel is most successful?
This depends on my mood. I love the bedroom in the morning when the sun comes in through the big beech tree in the garden, and the living room in the evening. The houses were designed with a balcony on the first floor, with a shelf just at the right height for resting a drink.

How have your design principles influenced your home?
Design is just part of my life. I don't feel I have applied design principles to the house. The house is not mine alone, it belongs to us, my family, my wife and my son. I am not solely responsible for the way it is. It is a function of family life and evolution. We have things here which are mine, things which belong to Corinna and some that belong to our son.

What is design?
Design is evolving all the time and with it a definition. Whatever is defined now will be out of date as culture changes, and with it expectations, needs and technology. Design is the lubricant between industry and the consumer of the product produced. It's the thing that makes industry's

product attractive to people. It uses a mostly subconsciously read language of signals to communicate.

How have your views on design changed since you began your career?
I now think of design as a business rather than an amateur pursuit.

What have you learnt?
I have learnt always to try to do and say what I truly believe rather than try to please the people I am working for. I've had to learn to trust my own judgment and state my case.

Who are your heroes?
There aren't any heroes in design. There are lots of people whose work I like and whom I admire, but a hero's role is saving lives and standing up to bullies, changing the world.

Where do you seek inspiration?
Inspiration comes from everywhere: art, film, conversation, hard work, sleep.

How do you begin working on a project?
By thinking about the criteria and the problem which needs to be solved.

What do you prefer to work with? Computer? Pencil? Pen?
People first, then a pencil, then a computer.

How do you reconcile design with consumerism?
I believe in quality.

What is the one thing that every home needs?
A roof and if there is such a thing as community, which helps to make a home, too.

What could you not live without?
Live? I would find life unbearable if I lost my wife or my baby or my sight. Work? Unfortunately, I could not work as easily without my computer, which is my whole office.

What kind of environment do you like working in?
A lively one.

How does it differ from your living space, if at all?
Not much in mood, but a work space needs to be more organized and efficient.

Describe an average day.
I don't often have average days, that's the best thing about my working life, the huge variety. One day I am in Denmark visiting the factory where Arne Jacobsen Egg chairs are made, two or three days later I might be in Istanbul at a factory producing wash basins.

What is important?
What is really important? In the design field, progress.

What are we getting right today?
It seems that it is always easier to say what we are getting wrong. But the beginnings of serious attempts to develop renewable energy sources, making it increasingly difficult to use our cars in cities, increases in fuel taxes, organic farming are things that we are getting right.

Nature or nurture?
I think that we as designers have to do anything we can to influence people,

individuals and companies, to produce products that either use less energy, are easily recyclable or last well and improve with age.

Should a home be 'a machine for living in'?
This is an outmoded modernist dictum. We are not cogs, therefore we don't need a machine to house us! As much as I like Le Corbusier, it is an overused, overrated statement taken out of context.

What is taste?
Taste is an amusing sense, like smell or hearing, which can be tuned and which changes constantly. It is a sense that recognizes sometimes very subtle signals; a way of inventing and recognizing signs distinguishing one tribe from another.

What's your favourite material to work with?
Light.

How do you feel you've made your mark?
Persistently and quietly.

If you were asked to give the world a single piece of advice, what would it be?
The world is so diverse that advice given to some would be misinterpreted by others and we would end up with clichés like 'live life to the full'.

What will the house of the future look like?
The British house of the future is unfortunately probably going to look like an ugly mix between a shrunken Georgian townhouse and a Tudor country one. But I don't think that what the house

of the future looks like is at all important, the issue is how is it built, what materials are used, how is it powered, how efficient is it and how comfortable is it to live in?

What's next?
What is next?

joseph holtzman

Where do you live?
New York City, in a one-bedroom apartment.

How did you find your home?
Through Feathered Nest, a rental agency.

How long have you lived there?
Over twenty years.

What was the starting point for its design?
A huge shoebox of a living room, with ugly ceiling beams.

Which room do you feel is most successful?
The three rooms are equally successful/unsuccessful.

How have your design principles influenced your home?
I discovered my design principles by decorating this home.

What is design?
Design is what I do. Please don't think about that.

How have your views on design changed since you began your career?
My design evolves; my sense of the creative process has stayed the same.

What have you learnt?
Many things.

Who are your heroes?
Christopher Dresser, Kent William, Todd Oldham, Richard Tuttle, any smart person under twenty-five.

Where do you seek inspiration?
It seeks me out.

How do you begin working on a project?
Some big idea comes along, usually while I'm in the bath.

What do you prefer to work with? Computer? Pencil? Pen?
I work with a computer-literate colleague. He pushes the buttons.

How do you reconcile design with consumerism?
I have great appreciation for material and workmanship, so it is hard for me to cater to mass taste. 'Good design' is only part of the story.

What is the one thing that every home needs?
Privacy.

What could you not live without?
Privacy.

What kind of environment do you like working in?
My apartment and adjoining office. (The two sort of run together.)

How does it differ from your living space?
See previous answer.

Describe an average day.
Stressful, hectic, too many people wanting my attention.

What is important?
**Feeling creative and
productive. Being the same.**

What are we getting right
today?
**We are beginning to get
beyond the modernist reflex.
We have a long way to go,
as current excesses show.**

Nature or nurture?
Beg pardon?

Should a home be 'a machine
for living in'?
**No. That sounds boring.
Maybe 'a machine for
refining perceptions in'.**

What is taste?
**Good or bad. Both a step up
from none.**

What's your favourite material
to work with?
Ideas.

How do you feel you've made
your mark?
With *Nest* magazine.

If you were asked to give the
world a single piece of advice,
what would it be?
**Find things out for yourself.
Ask questions.**

What will the house of the
future look like?
Whose house?

What's next?
**I'd like to see designers
come up with a new
vocabulary of ornament,
like Christopher Dresser
did. Form without ornament
is like sex without love.**

enzo mari

Where do you live?
In Milan, near the churches of Sant'Ambrogio and Santa Maria delle Grazie.

How did you find your home?
While I was wandering around house-hunting, I caught sight of a courtyard with trees, and a terrace covered with a huge wisteria. As I was thinking that I would like to live there, I spotted the concierge putting up a small 10 cm² blue card. It read 'For Sale' in small writing. I went in and bought it for a relatively small amount.

How long have you lived there?
Thirty-six years.

What was the starting point for its design?
A long passage with small rooms, leading out on to the terrace.

Which room do you feel is the most successful?
The terrace.

How have your design principles influenced your home?
From a general point of view, which encompasses everything I know, and includes personal rules, and is sensitive to my unconscious impulses.

What is design?
Nowadays, the word 'design' has taken on an awful meaning. This is why I prefer the word 'disegno', which was considered to be the first among the arts during the Italian Renaissance.

How have your views on design changed since you began your career?
In 1950, the word 'design' meant conceiving a new world based on the dignity of work. Today, its meaning has been totally twisted.

What have you learnt?
I continue to learn. This line of work constantly deepens my understanding that not only are a large proportion of people losing their human dignity, but also of the subtle reasons that are leading to this loss.

Who are your heroes?
Simple folk defending their own dignity.

Where do you seek inspiration?
In the archetypes of doing and thinking.

How do you begin working on a project?
By trying to understand and define its purpose. A project works when its purpose is clarified.

What do you prefer to work with? Computer? Pencil? Pen?
With a pencil.

How do you reconcile design with consumerism?
Consumerism is based on the rapid obsolescence of each form. For this reason, I try to counter it by realizing forms that won't go out of fashion.

What is the one thing that every home needs?
The happy serenity of the people who live in it.

What could you not live without?
What I see out of the window is of the utmost importance to me.

What kind of environment do you like working in?
An environment that is large and on an exaggerated scale – for example, an empty industrial unit, with an overhead crane. This would allow me to project my work in lots of ways.

How does it differ from your living space, if at all?
In that my studio, in which I have worked for over forty years, is a jumble of files, models and materials.

Describe an average day.
Four trips on foot between my house and my studio which is eight kilometres in total.

What is important?
To try to work and live in a way that is not alienating.

What are we getting right today?
A lot, potentially.

Nature or nurture?
What's the difference?

Should a home be 'a machine for living in'?
I don't like the word 'machine'. If the words 'to live' are enough in themselves they are confined, they become a nightmare.

What is taste?
From the dictionary, 'instinctive judgment of aesthetic values'. It is necessary to add to this, if the instinct derives from a passionate knowledge of the early texts, the great archetypes of the plastic culture.

What's your favourite material to work with?
All of them. I choose whatever is right and necessary.

How do you feel you've made your mark?
I must admit that I've always tried to do that. It's up to others to judge for themselves.

If you were asked to give the world a single piece of advice, what would it be?
Just one? What a question! God has suggested ten. It would be sufficient to interpret them from a layman's point of view, putting a modern spin on them. For example, honour your father and mother, the foundation of our knowledge. Do not commit impure acts. Do not create fashionable design.

What will the house of the future look like?
What will the future be like?

What's next?
There won't be any 'future' if the values we use as points of reference continue to be free time, tourism, the personal computer, the Internet, technology, creativity based on ignorance and the global market.

david mellor

Where do you live?
The Peak National Park in Derbyshire in a converted industrial building alongside my purpose-designed cutlery factory, which was once the village gasworks.

How did you find your home?
By chance. We came across a redundant gasworks in a marvellous rural site. I have always believed in integrating living and working in one place.

How long have you lived there?
Fourteen and a half years.

What was the starting point for its design?
Our home was once the Retort House (a stone-built gas-processing building). We extended this with a further living area that I designed.

Which room do you feel is most successful?
The large first-floor living area incorporating kitchen and dining table as well as comfortable seating, with a terrific view out over the hills.

How have your design principles influenced your home?
I am a maker and many of the elements in my home have been specifically designed and made in my own workshops, e.g., the stainless steel spiral staircase (we have a duplicate in our house in Italy!).

What is design?
A combination of functional efficiency and aesthetic appeal.

How have your views on design changed since you began your career?
Design is constantly evolving as one grows older, sees more and learns more. But I still look back on some of my earliest designs, for example, Pride cutlery, with great pleasure.

What have you learnt?
I have learnt a great deal from having my own shops, in terms of awareness of people's needs and aesthetic response. People tend to appreciate the best you put before them!

Who are your heroes?
Christopher Dresser, the pioneering metalworker of the Victorian period, and Alvar Aalto, the great Finnish architect and designer.

Where do you seek inspiration?
The astonishing collections of the Victoria and Albert Museum in London, of which I was a trustee for many years.

How do you begin working on a project?
I develop my designs three dimensionally, perfecting the model to arrive at a prototype.

What do you prefer to work with? Computer? Pencil? Pen?
None of these. I like to work directly with the metal in arriving at my designs.

How do you reconcile design with consumerism?
No problem. I like my designs to be usable and appreciated by my public.

What is the one thing that every home needs?
Cutlery!

What could you not live without?
My wife, my cat.

What kind of environment do you like working in?
Uncluttered.

How does it differ from your living space?
It doesn't. The two are completely interrelated.

Describe an average day.
Focused entirely around my work – product development, selection

of shop merchandise, with
intervals for very good food.

What is important?
My surroundings.

What are we getting right
today?
**Much more public
understanding of the
modern compared with
even ten years ago.**

Nature or nurture?
**Design is instinctive,
but perfectible by good
teaching and wide
observation.**

Should a home be 'a machine
for living in'?
Yes, of course.

What is taste?
You know when you see it.

What's your favourite material
to work with?
Metal.

How do you feel you've made
your mark?
**With a few nice shops and
a few dozen good designs
which have stood the test
of time.**

If you were asked to give the
world a single piece of advice,
what would it be?
Keep trying.

What will the house of the
future look like?
Anybody's guess.

What's next?
More knives and forks!

jay osgerby

Where do you live?
Brockley, London.

How did you find your home?
Through an estate agent.

How long have you lived there?
A year and a half.

What was the starting point for its design?
The need for a larger, open-plan floor plate and a desire to see the garden from the front door. We also wanted to be able to talk to friends as we cooked.

Which room do you feel is most successful?
The ground floor is one big room and the nicest space in the house.

How have your design principles influenced your home?
The design of the house is common sense for anyone who wants a light, airy space. The selection of furniture and objects reflects my design principles more clearly.

What is design?
A process of personal creation based on a lifetime of spaces, objects and experiences.

How have your views on design changed since you began your career?
They haven't.

What have you learnt?
French.

Who are your heroes?
My grandparents.

Where do you seek inspiration?
Flea markets, junk shops and aircraft hangers.

How do you begin working on a project?
By making a coffee.

What do you prefer to work with? Computer? Pencil? Pen?
Pen.

How do you reconcile design with consumerism?
Design better, buy less and recycle it.

What is the one thing that every home needs?
A family.

What could you not live without?
My family.

What kind of environment do you like working in?
On a tidy table in a messy room.

How does it differ from your living space, if at all?
The table is rarely tidy.

Describe an average day.
Coffee, work, coffee, work, lunch, work, coffee, work, wine, work…more wine.

What is important?
Trigonometry and the planets.

What are we getting right today?
iTunes.

Nature or nurture?
Nature.

Should a home be 'a machine for living in'?
A home shouldn't smell of oil.

What is taste?
A reaction to an object, environment or image that is judged against a mental library of do's and don'ts built up through a lifetime.

What's your favourite material to work with?
Any material that can really be manipulated.

How do you feel you've made your mark?
I don't think I have yet.

If you were asked to give the world a single piece of advice, what would it be?
Don't stop turning.

What will the house of the future look like?
A tree house.

What's next?
Wine.

dieter rams

Where do you live?
I live with my wife in a house in Kronberg, just outside Frankfurt.

How did you find your home?
I didn't, I designed and oversaw the building myself on land purchased by Braun. The house was erected and furnished according to my own ideas.

How long have you lived there?
Since 1971.

What was the starting point for its design?
I was both stimulated and inspired by a housing development in Halen, near Bern in Switzerland, that the architects Atelier Five designed.

Which room do you feel is most successful?
My work space.

How have your design principles influenced your home?
Based on my experience as a designer, I have distilled

the essentials of my design philosophy into ten points. It was impossible for me not to be influenced by these principles in the design of my own home. My ten points are listed below.

What is design?
**Good design is innovative.
Good design makes a product useful.
Good design is aesthetic.
Good design makes a product understandable.
Good design is honest.
Good design is unobtrusive.
Good design is long lasting.
Good design is thorough down to the last detail.
Good design is environmentally friendly.
Good design is as little design as possible.**

How have your views on design changed since you began your career?
In general, my views have not changed.

What have you learnt?
One never stops learning.

Who are your heroes?
Mies van der Rohe and entrepreneurs such as Adriano Olivetti and Erwin Braun.

Where do you seek inspiration?
Inspiration can come from everywhere. One has to keep one's eyes and ears wide open.

How do you begin working on a project?
**1 Thinking
2 Sketching
3 Three-dimensional models**

What do you prefer to work with? Computer? Pencil? Pen?
I refuse to use a computer. I prefer to draw by hand in pen and occasionally I use a pencil.

How do you reconcile design with consumerism?
I hope that the 'purchase attraction' aesthetic upon which design today is almost exclusively based, and which only fuels the destructive product

extravagance, will give way to an aesthetic that supports long-term use and the conservation of resources.

What is the one thing that every home needs?
People living there, but first of all, doors and windows.

What could you not live without?
The Second World War and the years that followed have taught me that one can live with what is available.

What kind of environment do you like working in?
My own.

How does it differ from your living space?
There is no difference.

Describe an average day.
Not sitting on a park bench.

What is important?
To eliminate the unimportant.

What are we getting right
today?
Not much.

Nature or nurture?
**Specific environment under
specific conditions.**

Should a home be 'a machine
for living in'?
**Maybe our next home, on
another planet.**

What is taste?
**Something you cannot learn
by being taught.**

What's your favourite material
to work with?
**I like to work with
combinations of materials.**

How do you feel you've made
your mark?
**With my credo 'less but
better'.**

If you were asked to give the
world a single piece of advice,
what would it be?
**Stop continually inventing
another uproar, racket or
sensation.**

What will the house of the
future look like?
**Looking into the future
is still as unsettling,
complicated and confusing
as it was when the Oracle
of Delphi gave its prognosis,
prediction and forecasts.**

What's next?
See above.

karim rashid

Where do you live?
I live in New York City. I have a 200 sq m loft that is above my office in Chelsea.

How did you find your home?
I found my loft building after looking at over 100 properties in Manhattan over a period of a year, whereas I found my country house on the Internet in one afternoon.

How long have you lived there?
Four blissful years.

What was the starting point for its design?
I bought half of a four-storey building. I have the basement and first floor as my design studio and the second floor is my loft.

Which room do you feel is most successful?
I love the bathroom. I think today's fixtures are all so formal and part of that 'stylized tasteful bullshit'. We need rubber baths; rubber watertight floors; lighting that can imitate daylight, halogen, fluorescent, the disco, the moonlight, at the flick of a switch. We need 'Smart Bathrooms' that diagnose your health through your faeces, a floor that diagnoses your weight, your heartbeat and vital signs, and a mirror that gives you digital feedback on your health, appearance, etc. The sinks, toilet, lights and everything should be automatic (like my personal bathroom) with no hand contact and, of course, a perpetual customizable aroma.

How have your design principles influenced your home?
My teaching ranges from phenomenology to philosophy to human behaviour, anthropology and social issues. I also teach 'form follows subject' – the subject is what you must lay concrete on, to inform form. Form follows fluid is a metaphor for form being amicable to our human psyche; that form can be friendly, part of us, part of our 'natural landscape'.

I also say 'more is more' because I hate modernism, minimalism, bullshit 'taste' and so called 'classic'. To work in the moment is to work in the first order – no preconceptions, no biases, no forced 'style' because 'styles' are the past.

What is design?
Design is our entire built landscape. Design is crucial to our domestic environments, to our modes of transportation, to our hospitals, our products. Design is everywhere. Sadly 90% of it is awful. Everything needs to be designed from our aeroplane interiors to our shampoo bottles. We need to beautify this planet in every aspect, in every corner of the earth.

How have your views on design changed since you began your career?
We are living in a fantastic time because there is a blurring of the boundaries and categories in design and our built environment for the first time. I was brought up in a household where my father designed everything, from my mother's clothes to the furniture to television and film sets. I think I decided when I ran my own practice that I would stay as pluralist as possible, kind of like a Warhol factory, or an Eames factory, and to try to do cross-discipline kinds of things. I am designing products, jewelry, eyeglasses, radios, furniture, interiors, architecture, painting, fashion and ambient music. The common thread of all these disciplines is industry. They are all part of the world of Industrial Design, so in fact I am a cultural shaper.

What have you learnt?
In the excrescence of goods and the system of objects, the possibility of over consuming, of accumulation, and immediate satisfaction of consumption is dangerous. We surround ourselves in life with effigies, objects, products to find meaning in our existence and to create a sense of memory, of presence and of belonging. But we also consume to occupy time and to fulfil some strange need of reward and ego. We will forever have objects in our world, and I am not advocating that we should not consume or that we should not have 'things', but to be hyperconscious of our things, love and enjoy them. If not, do without them.

Who are your heroes?
My parents were quite cosmopolitan and my father bought me a book on Raymond Loewy when I was eleven years of age. I also admired so many artists from all the books scattered in the house. I loved Andy Warhol, Aleksandr Mikhailovich Rodchenko, Pablo Picasso, Alexander Calder, Joan Miró, Le Corbusier, Dec Chirac, David Hockney, YSL, Roy Frowick Halston, Pierre Cardin, and so many other artists who were pluralists. Design, art, architecture, fashion and film. It was all the same to me – creation, beauty and communication.

Where do you seek inspiration?
I am inspired by my childhood, my education, by all of the teachers I have ever had, by every project I have worked on, by every city I have travelled to, by every book I have read, by every art show I have seen, by every song I have heard, by every smell, every taste, sight, sound and feeling.

How do you begin working on a project?
When I meet with a client, I immediately have several ideas which I sketch right after the meeting. I keep sketching over and over. Then I put together several of my senior staff and explain the project, the concepts and they start to develop the concepts digitally with 3-D modelling programs. Then I review it – or keep thinking about the project, I research the possibility of the behavioural issues, new materials, new technologies, etc., and I share this information with my staff. In turn, I have people in the office researching the same pragmatic issues and getting virtual, solid or real models produced. Each project actually has a very different process, sometimes vertical, sometimes linear, sometimes hypertextual. I used to do the drafting, the rendering, the engineering, the sketching and the entire process, but these days I do not have the time.

What do you prefer to work with? Computer? Pencil? Pen?
I am an advocate of digital technology. It is the instrument for the new Tower of Babel phenomena. The world started as one dialect, one religion, one culture and then it built the Tower of Babel to reach utopia (heaven, nirvana, god). But god would not allow the folk to reach him or the heavens so he gave everyone a diverse tongue, a diverse culture, diverse beliefs so they could not communicate. This is the beginning of the world as we know it, but we are returning to that global constellation – utopia.

How do you reconcile design with consumerism?
Industrial design was founded on capitalism. The idea of mass producing commodities at accessible prices and distributing them globally was the origin of this profession. They are capital goods for consumption and economic growth. Without industry there is no industrial design. I think at one point, postmodernism became design for design's sake. And, in turn, our goods in everyday life lacked meaning, poetry, aesthetics and function. Ever since I was a child I wondered why there couldn't be a more democratic design that everyone could enjoy. But today, design can sell. Manufacturers can make good business from design. I think we've arrived at an age when design can participate in popular culture and be part of everyday life. Design is no longer for the elite!

What is the one thing that every home needs?
Ideally I would like to see every home as a 'SMART' home where everything is automated – everything is intelligent; no light switches, no taps to touch, no doors to open, no thermostats to adjust, no obstacles. A smart wardrobe that tells you what you have clean. A smart kitchen that scans the upc codes of your food, tells you when things are bad and even gives you meal-combination choices, where extra oxygen is piped through the space, where scents are electronically controlled and highly energetic amorphous flexible spaces are spiritual and ephemeral.

What could you not live without?
Beauty, love and intellect.

What kind of environment do you like working in?
I see a re-arrangeable system to create a 'built-in' lounge that grows from the ground, an extension of the natural landscape to the artificial landscape. All the notions of objects of comfort are dispelled and are replaced by an environment rising out of the ground. The continuous white field is surrounded by a field of fluorescence to allude to the world of technology, to digital space and arbiters, as a refuge from 'infotrophy'.

How does it differ from your living space?
I love my loft. It is a paradisiacal lacuna from the non-stop day-to-day high-energy world in which I work, forever changing, forever dynamic, and forever now. I think a living space needs flexible, customizable, variable affordances. I think the future is about personalization. Our domestic space sets a stage for a non-stop amorphous scape that denotes a world with no boundaries. I see a space that extends itself via plastic organic modules of repetition, a continuum of surface based on a conventional Cartesian grid of the floor. 'Pleasurescape'

is a metaphor for a continuous world, a neutral landscape and an undulating surface that is re-configurable and re-sizeable ad infinitum. Where architecture and furniture blur, where objects metamorphose into space.

Describe an average day.
Generally, I am travelling, designing and co-ordinating projects from the road. I love being on planes where I can really focus on projects. I can fill a sketchpad on a single European flight (about 100 pages). I write proposals, answer press questions, strategize, develop ideas, directions and dream about what I really want to do – not what I think I must do. I travel about 180 days a year. I have crazy days in the office. I must sleep 7$^{1}/_{2}$ hours exactly, or I have trouble performing. I wake up at 8 am, brew the strongest fresh cup of espresso, answer all my e-mails (usually European or Japanese at that time), then go down to the office. I review issues with my office manager, answer more e-mails, write articles, proposals, etc., then look at the list of projects. I meet with each one of my staff (I probably review/work on the design of 20 projects in a day, I have about 40 projects going on so I manage to get to each project every other day). I have two or three client meetings, salade niçoise almost every day and a soy shake, drink four strong coffees and one late afternoon decaf and I keep going until about 8 pm.

Then I either go to the gym, go out for dinner or go to an opening. I try not to work past 10 pm because I work seven days a week. I perpetually multi-task.

What is important?
All relationships are collaborative. If I work with a company then the expectation is a marriage of my brand, vision and ideas with their company culture. Generally, companies I work with or who come to me have a very similar philosophy and this is when it really works well. It is a myth that designers have an idea and a company produces it. The real work is this collaborative merging of minds, vision and ideology. It took me many years to learn that the only time it works is when you have the right relationship and relationships are everything in life, love, business, friendship and support.

What are we getting right today?
We are finally starting to realize that in order to exist NOW you must live in the world NOW, which means to live in contemporaneity and to let go of the past, to do away with nostalgia, and preconceptions. Living now is to be free.

Nature or nurture?
Man does not have a great relationship with nature. In fact, man opposes nature. Take a walk in the park. But leave the park – respect nature, do not destroy it.

Should a home be 'a machine for living in'?
Yes. In a post-industrial house our conditions will be more relaxed, not rigid, softer, where our experiences will be more hypertextual and less linear. It is not a coincidence that the driving force behind the changing and ever-shifting global lifestyles is becoming more casual, more relaxed, softer and smarter. Organic systems will change our paradigms and 'Organomics' (a term I coined for the study of ergonomics and organic form) may shape the objects with touch every day.

What is taste?
All artists want to change the world, I just happened to say it. I am interested in rethinking the banal, changing our commodity landscape and proposing new objects for new behaviours and for diverse markets. I am interested in democratizing design, I am interested in getting the public to live now and I am trying to do away with class, elitism, mass and conventions. I am trying to irradiate high art and low art. I see one beautiful seamless world with no racial differences. I hate the word taste. I believe that design is extremely consequential to our daily lives where we impact physical, physiological and sociological behaviour and set up conditions of human experience. I give birth to a multitude of things, both material and immaterial. These things can shape our lives. I want to change the world.

What's your favourite material to work with?
Although I work with all materials, I love plastic. Plastics are outperforming any natural material and have phenomenal property possibilities and opportunities.

How do you feel you've made your mark?
I am a household name in New York because I speak, write, lecture, design, etc. I am in the public realm. I do not believe design is elitist. I have visited every shopping mall in America and I focus on the public, not the design community.

If you were asked to give the world a single piece of advice, what would it be?
Obsession, passion, perseverance, consistency and talent. A desire to work with companies, to collaborate. Design is collaboration, not just personal expression.

What will the house of the future look like?
I think that in the future we will own nothing. We will create a hyper-consumptive, forever dynamic and ever-vast changing human condition, where everything will be cyclic, sustainable, biodegradable and seamless. This is utopia, this is freedom, this is nirvana.

What's next?
I would love to design everything that we come into contact with as human beings, especially when they have a large impact on our psyche and experiences. There is so much to do. I want to be part of the entire world, working in every country, touching the souls of everyone. I want to be smarter, faster, stronger.

jerszy seymour

Where do you live?
Milan.

How did you find your home?
A newspaper ad.

How long have you lived there?
Four years.

What was the starting point for its design?
Domestic anarchy.

Which room do you feel is most successful?
The big one.

How have your design principles influenced your home?
My home influences my work. It is where I relax and nurture my thoughts.

What is design?
To be curious. Design is many things, the question for me is not 'what is design?', but 'why design?'

How have your views on design changed since you began your career?
My views haven't changed, in fact I am more convinced.

What have you learnt?
To enjoy differences.

Who are your heroes?
Peter Sellers and Che Guevara.

Where do you seek inspiration?
In dark corners.

How do you begin working on a project?
With lots of questions.

What do you prefer to work with? Computer? Pencil? Pen?
Everything.

How do you reconcile design with consumerism?
I think the question is, 'How do we reconcile consumerism with society?' And, 'How do we make a consumerism which is balanced?'

What is the one thing that every home needs?
A roof and a bed.

What could you not live without?
Love.

What kind of environment do you like working in?
Dark and cave-like.

How does it differ from your living space, if at all?
It doesn't.

Describe an average day.
Freestyle.

What is important?
You.

What are we getting right today?
Protesting against corporate-run governments and fighting for the rights of the global people.

Nature or Nurture?
Both.

Should a home be 'a machine for living in'?
No.

What is taste?
Very personal.

What's your favourite material to work with?
Materials that can give surprises.

How do you feel you've made your mark?
I don't know, time will tell.

If you were asked to give the world a single piece of advice, what would it be?
Fuck.

What will the house of the future look like?
Dark and cave-like, but with some holes in the ceiling to let in some sunlight.

What's next?
Global democracy or anarchy.

ali tayar

Where do you live?
In between apartments –
in other words, in a state
of glorified homelessness.
In any case, I always think
of my office/studio in the
meatpacking district of
Manhattan as being in some
sense my true home, the
place that most deeply
bears my imprint. And since
I've designed a wide range
of shelving systems over
the years gradually most
of my books have also come
to live in the studio.

How did you find your home?
As a sublet from a sound
studio. It was advertised on
small photocopied sheets
in the neighbourhood as
they were trying to keep
it somewhat in the dark
from the landlords.

How long have you lived there?
After a twilight zone, which
lasted five years as semi-
legal tenants, we have just
signed a lease with the
owners.

**What was the starting point for
its design?**
The space is mostly lit by
two large skylights, which
provide a wonderful light
and a sense of seclusion
from the city. Their location
dictated the area used for
meetings, defined by a
large, bent plywood table,
an entrance area with two
mid-century slipper chairs
and the work area, which
consists of mdf panels
on filing cabinets. As new
prototypes arrive we
reshuffle the pieces so that
we give the newcomer a
prominent place. The older
designs sometimes have
to disappear into a small
storage area in the back of
the studio or get suspended
from the wall.

**Which room do you feel is most
successful?**
I only have one big space,
which gets tidied up before
a visit from a friend, a
new client, a curator or
a journalist. I then slowly
expand my paperwork over
all available surfaces until
the next such visit.

**How have your design principles
influenced your home?**
It could be said that my
design principles live in
my studio/home.

What is design?
My background is in
architecture and engineering
design. I hold degrees from
the University of Stuttgart
and MIT. After graduation
I joined an engineering firm
where I worked on aeroplane
hangars for the US Airforce.
Design for me primarily
consists of applying
engineering principles
to the scale of furniture.
My interest in production
processes also goes back to
my training in prefabrication
and architecture. In my
forms I try to reconcile the
often contradictory
requirements of production
processes with diagrams
of the flow of forces.

**How have your views on design
changed since you began your
career?**
Rather than using the word
'changed' I would say that
my views have evolved.
I used to design with the
single-minded goal of
having pieces in production
– a kind of obsession to
repeat the experiences
of mid-century American
designers. Over the years
I've moved towards a more
playful attitude of exploring
different modes of
production, from a 3D-
printed resin candleholder,
to re-creating paper cups
in sterling silver by hand
in Kathmandu.

What have you learnt?
The most important thing
is to keep working on new
stuff. The last man standing
will win.

Who are your heroes?
Antonio Gaudi for his
structural expressionism
and Jean Prouve for his use
of production processes. I
also admire Prouve for
making his political
convictions the basis of his
entire career. Among my
contemporaries I admire
Jasper Morrison for being
so consistent.

Where do you seek inspiration?
I've been inspired by both
discarded industrial objects
and the depiction of hand-
held torches in a film or
anything in between.
Discussions with Ellen
Levy, my business partner,
always help me to see the
problem and/or the solution
clearly.

**How do you begin working on
a project?**
I usually start thinking of
a structural principle and a
specific production process
for a given task. I always
discuss my ideas with Attila
Rona, our structural
engineer. As in standard
architectural practice,
my design work is defined
by my collaboration with
a structural engineer.

What do you prefer to work with? Computer? Pencil? Pen?
I start out with sketches, which I keep making throughout the project. I try to resolve all constructive details in sketch format. This is something I picked up from studying Prouve's work. We then work on the computer.

How do you reconcile design with consumerism?
Having grown up with left-wing parents, my immediate response would be to condemn consumerism. On the other hand, if I'm honest, I look forward to the day my designs will cover the shelves of the store Target.

What is the one thing that every home needs?
'Love', to quote John Lennon.

What could you not live without?
It seemed that I might not have been able to live without this sketchbook I had grown attached to. Unfortunately, the company stopped manufacturing it and I continue to live.

What kind of environment do you like working in?
Messy!

How does it differ from your living space?
My living space will be organized, when I have one.

Describe an average day.
Coffee, gym, work, talk to Roy (a client), talk to Roy (a client), talk to Roy (a client), a drink, Law and Order, sleep.

What is important?
Doing whatever I am interested in doing without having to worry about survival.

What are we getting right today?
Very little.

Nature or nurture?
Having been exposed to 'good' German educators for twelve years of my schooling, I'd vote for nurture.

Should a home be 'a machine for living in'?
Preferably not (see my answer to 'What will the house of the future look like?') and certainly not a dwelling unit.

What is taste?
Whatever you feel while eating a good dessert.

What's your favourite material to work with?
More than specific materials what interests me are processes, trying out the widest range possible, from handcrafted to 3D-computer printed.

How do you feel you've made your mark?
Possibly by tweaking a few old ideas about production and structural expression a step further.

If you were asked to give the world a single piece of advice, what would it be?
The enlightenment was a good period.

What will the house of the future look like?
We are revisiting the ideals and ideas of modernism, hopefully having learned from its shortcomings.

What's next?
More of the same, until I get really good at it.

terence woodgate

Where do you live?
Just outside the beautiful medieval village of Mayfield in East Sussex, in a converted sanatorium that used to serve Mayfield College, an old public school which is now closed.

How did you find your home?
In a newspaper advertisement – it was the very first house we saw in the area.

How long have you lived there?
Nine years.

What was the starting point for its design?
A conversation with Sally Mackereth, a friend who is a partner in the architectural practice, Wells Mackereth. Sally came down to Mayfield and confirmed the potential I had seen in the house. It had already been converted but not very well, so we started by gutting the whole building. Together with James Wells, Sally did a superb job; it is a house that really works.

Which room do you feel is most successful?
The main living room. It's a big space, with a high ceiling, but is really comfortable, mainly due to the open log fire and the big sofa. Sitting by the fire in the winter with a bottle of wine is heaven.

How have your design principles influenced your home?
I am a fan of making geometry fit without compromising comfort.

What is design?
For me it is the fusion of art and science. Form following what I want it to be! It might follow the function, it might not; I decide, not some manifesto. The best designs are a joy to use and to look at. Neither should compromise the other.

How have your views on design changed since you began your career?
I think my work has become warmer and softer.

What have you learnt?
To wait a while, to take my time and let the work mature, but most of all to care.

Who are your heroes?
Mahatma Gandhi, Jackson Pollock, Donald Judd, Ben Nicholson and Charles Eames.

Where do you seek inspiration?
Everywhere. This comes back to my definition of design; it can come from the sculpture of Anthony Caro, for example, or the carbon-fibre suspension of the Williams Formula One racing car. Better to look outside of your discipline for inspiration.